THE BEING IN THE WORLD

TESKO

THE BEING IN THE WORLD

The Being, the Self, and the Self-within-the-self

BEN WOOD JOHNSON

TESKO

Copyright © 2022 by
Tesko Publishing

Copyright © 2012 by BAW
330 W. Main Street #214, Middletown, PA 17057

All rights reserved. No part of this publication may be reproduced, distributed, or transmitted in any form or by any means, including photocopying, recording, or other electronic or mechanical methods, or by any information storage and retrieval system without the prior written permission of the publisher, except in the case of very brief quotations embodied in critical reviews and certain other noncommercial uses permitted by copyright law.

Johnson, Wood Ben, 1975—

    The Being in the World / Ben Wood Johnson.

    p. cm.

Includes notes and index.

ISBN-13: 978-1-948600-41-5 (pbk: permanent paper)
ISBN-10: 1-948600-41-2

1. Philosophy, existentialism/human ontology—United States. 2. Phenomenology—United States. 3. Humanism—United States.

The information illustrated in this book was compiled for a school project.

The analysis is based on class notes and other materials.

Tesko Publishing

Cover Illustration Wood Oliver

For Fiate Widmark Patrick

Contents

Preface	*xiii*
Introduction	*1*
Section One: Misreading of the Man	
1. Two-Dimensional Beings	**9**
A False Duality	12
Being Robotized	13
2. Three-Dimensional Beings	**17**
The Roots of Human Existence	18
The Nature of Existence	20
Section Two: Assessing Self-Awareness	
3. Being Aware of Yourself	**25**
The Ability to Think	26
Every Being Ponders	28
Placing the Self in the World	29
4. Finding the Natural	**31**

Contents

Romanticizing the Self	33
Society as a Lethal Space	37
The Limits of Life in Society	39
5. We Are Ordinary Beings	**43**
Assessing Human Inventions	45
Understanding Humanness	48
Human Three-dimensionality	50

Section Three: Insanity and Consciousness

6. The Insanity Line	**57**
Denying the Self	58
A Lack of Certainty	60
Talking About the Self	62
Talking About Being	64
Let's Talk About Beingness	66
7. Human Consciousness	**69**
Watching Yourself Watching You	71
Searching for Yourself	74
Rejecting the Self	78

Section Four: Introspection and Awareness

8. An Incomplete Look	**83**
The Effects of Looking Around	85
A Three-Step Process	88
Freedom and Existentialism	90
9. The Self in a Mirror	**93**
Human Awareness	96

The Extent of Self-Awareness	97
Ignoring My Nature	99

Section One: Dimensionality and Awareness

10. A Three-Dimensional Entity — 103

The Being	104
The Self	105
The Self-Within-the-Self	107

11. Who Is (Truly) in the Mirror? — 109

Assessing the Concept of Beingness	111
Communicating With Nature	113

12. Controlling the Self — 117

The Pillar of Human Existence	119
Thinking and Human Essence	125
Conclusion	*127*
About the Author	*133*
Also by	*135*
Index	*137*

Contents

PREFACE

Living in a man's world can be a scary experience. Men can be so unkind. They can be so cruel towards their kind. Their hatred for each other can be incalculable; their disdain for one another can be unfathomable; their repulse for one another can be insuperable.

In a man's world, life can be unlivable. Existence can be painful. Life can be a drag. Striving to subsistence can be next to impossible. Endeavoring to exist beyond chance in a chancy milieu may prove artlessly demoralizing. It can be improbable. It can be impossible.

In places where ideas about antihumanism thrive, life may become a challenge for the life bearer. But the living experience is not a given. Subsisting is guaranteed to no one in this world. The precocity of humanness in a social hub can be more pervasive than you might imagine. The man must strive to stay alive. No matter what a man's circumstances might be, he must find a way to be.

How hard is it for a man to be in the world? How difficult it might be for a man to survive in a milieu designed to upend, though prematurely at times, his beingness? There are no definite answers to these questions.

The notion of survival is the trademark of the philosophical approach I echo throughout these pages. I will argue that the man must carry on. He must do so religiously and passionately. He must effort—tooth and nail (if need be)—to stay a whole. The man must survive no matter what his conditions might be. He must grasp the need to survive.

When the man canalizes the essence of his beingness, he must protect it. When the man comprehends the need for his beingness, he must do anything in his power to make it on his own and for his own. He must push the self to the brink. He must surmount any obstacles placed before him. He must deal with his problems with serenity and alacrity. He must effort [relentlessly] to survive by rights. He must not do so by claims, by chance, nor by choice. The man must be in the world. He must do so without being deprived of his beingness.

Being in the world epitomizes the worldview that human existence is not a given. The man must earn his place on earth. He must earn his rights to exist.

But few people grasp the nature of their own survival needs.

The man must grapple with his beingness. The man must gain insights about his reality. He must understand other living beings. The man must humble the self. He must face his vicissitudes with glee.

The man must realize that he will face hurdles in the world. He must face his destiny with pride. He must endure. He must persist. He must deal with his crucibles with a peace of mind. He must understand the limits of his life.

This book examines the epistemology of human survival. In it, I argue that the man must do anything in his power to be in the world. He must endeavor, come what may, to remain in the world. The man must simply be.

Presently, the conversation about beingness is non-existent. Most thinkers content themselves to rehash ideas that had been echoed centuries ago about humanness. It is not presumptuous. There is a dearth of an authentic epistemology about human beingness. Hence, there is a need to explore the nature of humanness.

It is equally important to echo that the world can be a dangerous place for a man. Artificial constraints may make it unnecessarily difficult for a man to exist on his own, by his own, and for his own sake. No matter what his circumstances might be, a man must preserve his beingness. He must thrive; he must suffer; he must survive.

I am stubborn about my existence. I am jealous of my beingness. I hope that you share that outlook. Perhaps this work will take you on a similar path.

This collection of essays discusses philosophical ideas, which you might find intriguing. The text is not unreasonably complicated. It does not contain long-winded jargons. The book is informative. It is a short, but also an easy, read. This is a plea in favor of self-preservation.

The book comprises twelve chapters, including an introduction and concluding thoughts. These chapters are succinct. They are cogently designed to meet your intellectual expectations. Each entry had been constructed to provide enough information to support the fundamental premise of the book.

The codicil outlined here is that men are in the world. They have all the means at their disposal to exist in this environment without serendipity. Before we go further in this interesting dialogue, let us explore chapter one, which elaborates on the notion of two-dimensionality in greater detail.

Good reading!
Ben Wood Johnson, Ph.D.
November 2022
Pennsylvania, USA

Introduction

How can the being [the man] be in the world? While this is an interesting question, I do not have a definitive answer. The nature of human beingness is complex. But that does not mean that we could not come up with a "convenient" explanation about why it might be of urgent need for a person to be.

While admitting the overbearing need to be, it is also worthy of note that it is not easy being on planet earth. Being is to exist by rights and not by privilege. Being is to exist by destiny and not by accident.

To be in this world is to manifest a presence that is far beyond a mere charnel state. The man must truly be in the world to be in such a place in the genuine sense of being. He must be in this milieu in the flesh; he must be there in the mind.

Is there a difference between being in the flesh and being in the mind? This question might seem lethargic. Why inquiring about the obvious, some might say? The argument could be made that to be in the flesh in the world, one must also be in the mind in this milieu. The opposite is also true. To be in the mind, one must also be in the flesh. Human existence depends on both states of being.

A person could not be in the flesh unless that individual is also in the mind. To transcend from the crystal and into the spiritual, the being must exist in both instances and simultaneously. This eventuality, if it were to be only conceivable or even plausible, would invariably contradict human understandings of themselves in the world. The foundation of a man's views about whom he is in the world is based on a dichotomous understanding of whom he could be. The man can perceive the self in the world by referencing his assessments of the possibility of not being present in that milieu. The certainty of a man is based on his own doubts.

The more you doubt, the more certain you become about your state of uncertainty, which corroborates any preconceived notions you might have developed about yourself and others in the world. Men exist in the world when they are certain that they could exist nowhere else. From a man's point of view, being in the world means to be certain that he is nowhere else but in the world itself. But this codicil is erroneous.

The Being in the World

Men are in the world. They are here; they are there. They are, I would say, despite themselves. Men are in the world regardless of their understanding of their presence in this environment.

Being in the world is not incumbent on any sense of self-worth, which men may or may not have about themselves. Being in the space, which is construed as the world, is not a choice. Instead, it is a factuality, which men have no say whether to remain there or whether to go elsewhere.

Men are stuck in the world. They do not need to be in two places at once to be certain of being in one space at a moment in time or space. In fact, the reality of men in the world is much more complex than men themselves realize. Indeed, men are in the world. But they are in many places and occupy many spaces at the same time. That fluidity is the trademark of existence.

Men exist in the world. Their capacity to meander back and forth between the real and the surreal is natural to the extent that men have an aesthetic sense of their own naturalness. The capacity of men to transcend from one place, albeit in the mind or in the spiritual, to the next, is nothing special. Men were designed to roam the world in which they exist. They can do so in the physical realm; they can do so in the charnel. They can do so on their own; they can do so for their kind; they can do so in their mind.

Introduction

Being in the world is not just a human reality. Being in this lieu is for every living entity, which acts and interacts with the natural. Hence, there is no secrecy in beingness, being that of a human being or that of any other beings.

To be in one place is to be in many places at once. That collection of beings makes up the reality of beingness itself. Being in the world is a point of reference to all the places in which the being is or has been. Hence, to be in the world is to be in every corner of the space, which makes up the place construed as the world itself. This is true wherever this world might be.

To be in the ocean, for example, is to have a whole-body experience in the water. Having a toe or a finger in the water could not be translated into being in the ocean as a whole. Being in the ocean means having an unabridged-body experience in the water, which makes up the deep-sea environment itself. A full-body experience anywhere in the world is not an ambivalence in nature, for the human body goes far beyond a dual presence in a specific milieu. There is more to humanity than the physical and the spiritual.

Men need not be on Mars or anywhere else to be or to exist outside the realm of happenstance. Men belong to planet Earth. They could only be here; that is, in the space known as earth. Men were born to exist in this milieu. The place of a man in the world is solidified at the mentioned locus. Thus, men could only be in the world as they have always known it, for they were designed to only be in such lieu.

Introduction

SECTION I

MISREADING OF THE MAN

1. Two-Dimensional Beings

A common understanding, which is misguided, is that a human being comprises two entities. There is the tangible person. This entity comprises flesh and bones. There is the spiritual person. This entity is known as the soul.

The soul, some would say, is the essence of the person. It is the foundation of the individual. The soul, many believe, offers the person a frame of reference in the landscape of life. Is there any truth to the preceding contentions? This chapter hopes to shed some light on the matter.

I do not subscribe to the idea that human beings, or any living being, could be only two-dimensional. It may be true that there are facets of a person who could only be understood through a two-dimensional lens. However, other facades of a living entity can be more subtle than a mere duality. Hence, there is more to life than a body and a soul.

Accepting that human beings only exist in a two-dimensional paradigm would be akin to accepting that human beings are fixed. That would also involve the following understanding. There would not be much difference between a person and a tree or a rock. The human being would be akin to a fixed object which would irrefutably have no essence, which would enjoy no autonomy, and which would have no sense of self. If men were fixed, that would also imply that they could not be a human being unless they had been born special beings.

If human beings were fixed entities, they would be in a state of inertia. Cartographically speaking, they would have a precise structure, which would always be discernible. Thus, one would not need exceptional skills to scrutinize a person in his most intrinsic sense. By that logic, a person could not be considered a mystery, which would require fundamental insights to decipher. We know that this is not the case at all. Human beings are among the most elusive creatures on earth.

No two men are the same. Similarly, no man experiences two consecutive seconds in the same way. Every second, every minute, every hour, every day, every week, every month, and every year, the man changes into a being whom even he does not (or could not) recognize.

Under the preceding articulations, a living being would have to be two-dimensional to be a whole. There would be the physical being (the person). There would also be the spiritual being (the soul). To what extent could this approach to humanity be correct? I would say…not at all. This view of human ontology, to put it this way, is misguided.

In my scrutiny of the man, I have found the preceding perspectives inaccurate. Although I do not have enough empirical evidence to corroborate this claim, I have studied myself. I have done so to the degree that I could do it. I have examined others. I have done this from afar. Every hint I have uncovered about the person, at least in the ontological realm, suggests that men are three-dimensional beings.

A *being* and a *soul, on* their own, are not enough to allow for a definitive panorama over humanity. Duality does not depict the nature of human beingness. There is more to the story of beingness than downgrading it to a mere dichotomy. There is more to humanness than consigning it to a mere physical matter.

* * *

A False Duality

The notion of duality does not depict the man in all his glory and flaws. The notion of two-dimensionality, which in most literary circles typifies popular—if not traditional—beliefs about humanness, is, by my understanding, untrue. This worldview does not—or could not—depict the man at the most intrinsic level; at least, it does not—or could not—do so as a whole. This idea does not—or could not—sketch out the reality of the *living entity*, which we could construe as a *man*.

If a living being—be it a person or else—were only two-dimensional, that entity would be fixed. The unit would not be alive. That singularity would be akin to an object. The being—in this case, the man—would not exist *on* his own or *for* his own sake.

If a life bearer (even if it were a person or any other living entity) were to exist based on the discretion of other entities (living or else), that being would lack any sense of self. He—or it—would be paralleled to the self. He—or it—would be automated by external entities. He—or it—would be moribund. He—or it—would be without automation. The life bearer (if we could call it that) would be akin to a machine.

The being would be similar in role and in action to an android-like instance. With a person, he would not enjoy any sense of freewill. That being would be the subject of the will of others. That entity would be a tool; he would be an object; he would be a contrivance designed to conduct a function. The being would be animated by his own design.

No being, at least known to humankind, meets the hitherto criteria, except for robots. However, we could not consider such creatures as living entities. Regardless of the intelligence a robot might have, it is the creation of men. It has no real essence; it is the product of another living—breathing—entity. A man could not pass down his sense of self to others. The same is true for nonliving entities.

* * *

BEING ROBOTIZED

A robot is an object. It is two-dimensional at its core beingness. This creation, regardless of its original constitution, has no essence beyond what had been granted to it by another.

A robot, in fact, is *a* matter of fact. It is, in the most vulgar sense, an unthinking entity. A robot has no nature. Thus, it has no natural state beyond what fate brings to its world. A living being is different.

Every living organism—be it a person or else—created in the natural, by the natural, or within the natural milieu itself is intrinsically un-streamlined. That entity is, in the most intrinsic sense, un-robotized; it is, in the most tangible sense, un-barbarized. Such entities are inherently humanistic.

Every living being is a part of the natural landscape. As a result, similar entities enjoy another dimension, which makes it possible for them to gauge the self towards other beings. That is why these living entities are three-dimensional in their core beingness. They are aware of their conditions. They understand their realities in the world in which they live.

An important trait separates a human being from other living entities. We could invoke their ability to ponder. We could contemplate their capacity to theorize between the material and the metaphysical as the foundation of their beingness.

Being able to philosophize is the quintessence of a person. But thinking is not just a human thing. That feature affords any living beings an advantage over non-living creatures within the milieu where they excogitate. The hitherto-remarked codicil presumes that only humans can think; at least, only they could do so introspectively.

A popular school of thought believes that humans are unique in the world. Some people are convinced that men are the only entities within the natural world that could produce thoughts. Could we say—at least with stubborn certainty—that this is the case? The obvious answer is no.

The notion that humans enjoy a special status in the world is not far-fetched. The peculiarity of the human species makes men akin to other entities on the planet Earth. This practicality is obvious only when considering the survival traits of a living being.

Are there extraordinary humans among us? If so, where are they? Are they somewhere? Are there superhumans in the world of men? Answers are unlikely in the affirmative.

Two-Dimensional Beings

2. Three-Dimensional Beings

As outlined in the previous chapter, duality is only a facet of beingness. It is not the essence of beingness itself. There is more to a body and a soul.

A person is more than a two-dimensional entity.[1] Every being—or every living being—is a three-dimensional instance, as opposed to being two-dimensional.[2] There is the being—the person or the physical entity. There is the self—the soul. It is the non-physical being, or it is the abstract entity.

There is the self-within-the-self. This entity could be understood as the inner self. That entity is the overseer of the self.[3]

---

[1] Chapter two elaborates further on this notion.

[2] Bear in mind that I use the terms person, being, and entity interchangeably throughout the document.

[3] Chapters 2, 5, 6, and 7 elaborate on the notion of three-dimensionality further.

A three-dimensionality contrivance is obvious in every living being. But beingness is not a unidirectional process. The concept of *a three-prong entity* could be considered the foundation of beingness. The same is true for humans. Being a three-dimensional entity is at the heart of humanness. This idea makes up the hurdles which human beings experience in their mundane life.

The three-dimensionality of beingness is not just a reality for human beings. That reality epitomizes the plight of all living beings. Three-dimensionality underpins the struggle for survival anywhere on Earth. Every living entity, as I would argue without reserve, is three-dimensional. This feature in men allows them to be. This is the essence of human existence.

What is human existence? How could we qualify it? How could we quantify that existence? Answers can be more complex than you think.

* * *

THE ROOTS OF HUMAN EXISTENCE

There is not a universal approach which would allow us to fathom (albeit intimately) the notion of existence. There is no way to contextualize human subsistence, though we could try. Nonetheless, we could not conduct this intellectual feat without evoking buzzwords or complicated verbiage.

Despite these limits, we could explore a link between a person's capacity to produce thoughts and a human's ability to process thoughts in a way that may transcend existence as the being has always known it. We could explore the individual's ability to find the appropriate means to prolong his existence. We could explore what catapults a person into this world.

The act of thinking is a conversation between the thinker and himself. It is a conversation between the thinker and other entities around him. In the natural space, thinking gives the thinker an edge. Through his thinking abilities, the thinker learns to communicate with the space where he breeds.

Overtime, the living being discovers the self. With a person, the entity learns valuable information about the environment in which he lives. This capacity helps the thinker to further his own existence.

No one knows what is happening in a thinker's mind. The subjective nature of humanness makes it impossible to find the roots of a thought. Therefore, we could not survey the roots of human existence without relying on subjective opinions, which could be a prejudice in their fundamental enunciation.

No one knows what is happening in another person's mind. No one can identify what it takes for a person to be. No one can explain what it takes for a man to be without evoking his own experience.

Despite the complex nature of the reality that men face in their daily living experience, we could rely on a subjective method to evaluate the conditions of the being. I would call this *philosophizing*. This approach is always intellectually relevant. It is that way regardless of what you might think that the notion itself means in the genuine sense of the concept of philosophizing.

Although we could rely on personal insights to prove the nature of human existence, it is important to note that theorizing is not a perfect science. There is no need to examine the existence of humans in the metaphysical realm. A lot has been said about humanness, at least in the ontological realm. Keep that in mind as you go through the remaining portion of the manuscript.

* * *

THE NATURE OF EXISTENCE

The ideas about the concept of existence are theoretical. There is no way to quantify the notion.

When we speak of existence, we could relate to our own plight. We could explore the idea of existence through the lens of a survivor.

I am a survivor. I have been alive for a long time. I have been surviving, though I have done so haphazardly, though I have done so here and there. My assessments of my living experience could help clarify the nature of your own pilgrimage.

To distinguish the being in all his intricacies, we must explore his mindset in the most intrinsic state. In this context, we could examine the nature of a thought. Valuating the characteristics of a human thinking process could help us make sense of it all.

Existence interacts with a person's ability to be, although it can clash with the person's capacity to think introspectively,[4] allowing the being to uncover a side of the self in a space, which would not have been possible otherwise. Thinking is the kernel of beingness. This is not just a human thing.

Every being, as long as that entity is alive or he— or it—wants to stay that way, shall think. This is the only way for the being—a person—to guarantee his survival beyond chance. A path to a certain state of being is not from this world. Human survival is more complex than most people realize.

---

[4] I use the term ability and capacity interchangeably in the document.

Three-Dimensional Being

There is more to human survival than relegated to a single physiological feature. There is more to the thought-producing process of a person than referring to it as a simple state of being at a specific moment. It is not enough to describe human survival as a mere exercise in producing a thought. Human existence is more complicated than this work could decipher.

The common belief is that thinking is a human characteristic. Only humans can think, they say. But how could this be? How could humans be certain that only—they—can think? This is a self-serving argument; it has no bearing on the real world. The above understanding does not concern the realities that other creatures make out in their quotidian.

If only human beings could think, then the world would have only humans in it. If only men could think, then only men would master the art of survival. If only men could think, then what would be the purpose of such attribution in them?

Before providing an answer, let us unravel the reality of human beingness in the world dominated by men and for the detriment of their kind. Let us explore the nature of beingness at the most intrinsic level. Let us make sense of the foundation of being. Let us examine the reason it might be important for a being (be it is a person or else) to strive tooth and nail to be in the world.

SECTION II

ASSESSING SELF-AWARENESS

3. Being Aware of Yourself

To be in the world is to be aware of the self in relation to other living entities. Awareness is an important facet of beingness. The man shall be aware of himself. He shall do so whether he finds himself in the wilderness or in a social setting.

The man shall strive to preserve his existence. He shall continue to be. He shall look for signs of any imminent danger to himself. He shall be cunning. He shall be incisive. He shall be smart. But the man shall do so only as a strategy to prolong his survival chances.

The man shall recognize that the social space could be more lethal to him than the natural environment could ever be. He shall understand that what nature limits, society—as an established actuality—restricts. Men shall concretize that the social milieu is a treacherous place. He shall also understand that such a terrain could never supersede the natural space. He shall develop a sure means to navigate his realities, be they social or otherwise. He shall deal with the environment.

The man shall master the survival means available in his surroundings. He shall deal with the limits that nature imposes on his beingness. He shall be attuned to the reality of his quotidian. He shall adjust himself. He shall supervise his conduct. He shall preserve his beingness. He shall be aware of himself. He must be mindful of other living beings.

Amid the tragedy of life, the man shall learn to stay. He shall learn to be beyond providence alone. He shall be a survivalist. He shall relish his nature.

The man shall recognize that he is the future of humanity. He shall grasp his duties in nature. He shall realize the urgent need to flourish. He shall know that he should endure. He shall face a world that had been designed to consume his beingness.

* * *

THE ABILITY TO THINK

How could the man realize the reality he faces at a moment? How could a man be without serendipity in a serendipitous world? The answer is that the man

The Being in the World

shall have a dialogue with himself. He shall think; he shall examine both himself and others.

While every human being enjoys the capacity (or the ability) to think, the function is not well understood. Human beings do not always comprehend—at least not at first—the nature of their existence. For a man to ride in this chaotic world outside of luck, he shall think.

The man shall recognize the reason—why—he thinks; at least he shall understand the reason he might have to do so. The man shall conceptualize the ramifications of his ability (or his capacity) to think. The man shall be conscious of the self. He shall be awoken by his reality.

The popular view is that only humans can think. Most people believe that a being's ability to think separates him from other beings. Is this always true?

Liking the realities human beings face in the natural world could help us unlock mysteries about human existence. Self-awareness is an important phase towards self-discovery. Every man shall engage in deep thinking. The man can think. This is an important aspect of being in the world. The man shall realize himself through the thinking process. This is how he gets insights about others. This is how the man discovers himself.

Being Aware of Yourself

* * *

EVERY BEING PONDERS

Thinking is not necessarily a human thing. Thus, every living entity can think. Of course, some do not do so in the same way humans do. It is irrefutable that every living being can think. This is the essence of existence.

Thinking is the foundation of man. It allows the being to be by rights and not by providence. This is precisely the reason that men can—and do—think.

As a bearer of life, thinking allows men to uncover the self in the natural. It gives them the ability to see the world for what it is and not how others depict it to them. Because of their ability to ponder, men enjoy the capacity to question the questionable. They can reflect on realities that might not be readily obvious to naked eyes.

Something else about human thinking is worth outlining further. Thinking allows the being—be it a person or else—to communicate with the self. As the being entertains himself, he learns about his realities. The man makes himself a place to be in this world.

Men can see themselves living harmoniously with both their kind and others. Men learn to develop strategies that would make it easier for them to overcome their obstacles in the milieu where they live. This allows men to achieve their goals, which would also reveal to men the need to carve a place for themselves in the natural space.

The man shall learn to withstand his quotidian. But he shall do so beyond good fortunes. He shall concretize this aim by constantly assessing his ability to ponder about the self and about others.

Every human can think. It is almost impossible not to do so. Thinking is the foundation of human beingness. In the same way, the capacity to ponder or the ability to reflect on the realities of the world is the essence of beingness.

* * *

PLACING THE SELF IN THE WORLD

The man shall commend his conditions in the world. The only way to do so is for the man to ponder about himself. The only way for the man to make sense of his situations is for him to think about his state of being. The only way for the man to think is that he shall realize himself.

When the man thinks, he might evade the hindrances that the natural might have placed on his way. Thinking makes it possible for the man to be in

Being Aware of Yourself

himself. It enables him to continue in this environment with certainty. Thinking makes the living experience bearable.

When the man thinks, he might develop tactics that would allow him to be on his own, by his own, and for his own. The man would know himself. He would know others. He would place himself rightfully among other living entities. The man would claim his own identity to be and to exist on his own and for his own sake.

It is urgent for the man to have a sense of self. He shall find himself. He shall find himself anytime, anywhere, and anyhow. As the man places the self-into the world, he becomes certain of his reality. The man may realize that he shall exist on his own. To concretize this feat, the man shall realize himself.

Being aware of yourself is important for the man. Being on his own and on his own would allow the man to exist as his nature intended. Doing so would allow the man to exist by rights and not by accident.

When the man realizes himself, he would be whole. This would allow the man to preserve his beingness. The man would do so in all instances. This is the quintessence of being in the world.

The man shall find a place to be. Doing so may be the most defying part of being in the world; it is not up to the man to be on his own. Let us consider the obstacles he may face to be in the world.

4. Finding the Natural

Insofar, we have discussed the need for the man to be. In previous chapters, we have outlined that for the man to be, he shall ponder; he shall deliberate about both the self and others. But he must do so at an introspective level.

From a fundamental standpoint, what is a thought? How does a person think? How do you know you are thinking?

The earlier queries are intellectually intriguing. I am not sure I could answer them objectively. Finding succinct answers about human thinking is difficult. Producing a thought is a complex function. But that does not mean that we could not speculate. That does not mean that we could not provide a thoughtful breakdown on humanness.

To explain the being, be it a humanoid or otherwise, we shall dig the nature of the natural. We shall also consider that nature is difficult to decipher from an empirical lens. Similarly, the link between the natural and the artificial (society) is not well understood. For some people, nature is an exogenous place. It shall be sought; it shall be imagined; it shall be envisaged.

Here, the understanding is that nature is a separate entity from the social environment. The natural place is a distinct milieu as opposed to the social space. Therefore, the natural and the social never intersect.

Most people believe that the natural milieu is lethal. This place is brutal; it is a dangerous space. A prevalent view is that there is a clear divide between the natural environment and the artificial hut. The belief is that the natural world is inhospitable; it is dangerous for humanity. No man shall venture into the natural world without taking the precautions to safeguard his life.

Many people see society and nature as separate entities. Some see the social sphere as a safer environment. The view is that a person would fare better in a social space than in a natural space. There, men could live in peace; they could live in harmony. The understanding here is that they could do so forever. Yet, this is not the case. This is a delusion.

* * *

Romanticizing the Self

Men have a romantic view of themselves. They feed misconceptions about whom they are in the natural world. Men believe to be gentle beings. Others see the species as righteous beings. Men are the direct heirs of God. They are rational beings. Men see themselves as innately good.

In the beginning of humankind's journey on earth, men themselves did not necessarily see their kind kindly. When men could think for themselves, they usually exposed a more cautious view of themselves. Men understood their malicious nature. Men learned to trust no men.

In the antiquity, most thinkers held a disparaging view of the humankind. They despised their kind; they reviled their habits of nurturing hatred toward one another. Jean-Jacques Rousseau, for instance, who had been recognized as a brilliant thinker, held a lesser esteem for the men of his epoch. Rousseau saw men as savages; and rightfully so, I might add. According to Rousseau, we shall suppress evil tendencies in men. We ought to suppress evil thoughts in them. For Rousseau, men are inherently bad. If not, they are prone to evil.

Viewpoints about men have changed. The collective understanding is that men are righteous in their core being. Most present-day theorists would share the notion that men are intrinsically good, they are rational beings. When men are acting bad, they are in bad faith; otherwise, they are acting out. Society shall instill order in them.

Most modern thinkers have a different take on the nature of men. Whether their approach is based on bad faith or else, they tend to see men as a victim of treacherous men. Put differently, men are not bad. Rather, some men are evil. Thus, there is a need to eradicate sinful men from the face of the earth. There is a need, from their vantage point, to deny wicked men the opportunity to be themselves. To do so, men (the righteous kind) must be both the judge and the executioners of their kind.

The pervading belief, which is nevertheless perverted at its core, is that some men are troublemakers. They must lose their freedom (or any sense thereof); they must be incarcerated; they must be deprived of life, liberty, and the pursuit of any sense of self, for this would undermine the peace and the tranquility of other men (the righteous kind).

A society, as the belief goes, is where men learn to become men. Some would even argue that a social space could bring the best out of men. But this view could not be further from the realities that men often face in their world. Society, I would contend, brings out the worst in men.

Another belief, which is riddled with perversions, is that every man should be civilized. Civilization is the foundation of adulthood. A civilized man is also a rational being. That level of purity, some are convinced, is attainable by every man and at the same time. Of course, this view is nonsensical; that is, it is that way no matter how you may spin this notion.

There is also a danger worth pointing out here. This attitude undermines men in their core being. It presumes that some men have an intrinsic inclination to be in a certain way. Thus, some men are righteous, while others are evil in their nature. This argument, to reiterate, is absurd.

Delusions about humanness are the foundation of our understanding of ourselves. They cause our misery. We distort our collective conditions by relying on our individual circumstances. What is for one man is never for another, at least not at the same time and in the same way.

Being in the world can be impossible for some men. It can become a burden, which few men could bear on their own and for their own sake. Being in the world can become a constant trial; it can be a permanent state of reclusion, which could be harmful to the man, at least eventually. This reality often contradicts our nature, as we were not designed to be other than how our nature intended.

Men were supposed to exist in the world in a chaotic manner. Considering that the world itself is random, life was also designed to be in the same way. There is no order in the living. Only the feeble mind can perceive only one aspect of the living, which is the one facet that the beholder of such a mind presumes to be to his best interest, notwithstanding the interests of the other, let alone the world itself. However, life was not designed to be a certain way.

Society ignores a man's nature. The only way men could be other than their nature ordained would be for them to renounce their—own—nature, which is impossible. This creates a constant struggle in the man to find the self in the world, thinking that he has lost himself in this midst of his incapacity to be as others want him to be.

The results of seeking to deny one's nature could have a devastating impact on the person's psyche. The man may be forced to be despite himself. He may be forced to exist haphazardly. He may be forced to be, according to others. He may be forced to become dependent on and of others. The man may be forced to be for others and for the benefit of others. The man may be forced to live in a depressing state. Life may become an incommensurable load.

* * *

SOCIETY AS A LETHAL SPACE

Artificial is deadly to men. But who created the social environment? Better yet, who created men? Are men a product of the social space where they live or is it the other way around? Answers are not definitive.

There are few places in the literature where one could read about the fallibility of men. There is a glorification of men. It is as if men were gods. They are expected to be perfect beings. When they fail, they shall receive harsh punishments for their behavior. This understanding is illogical.

Why men treat themselves as if they were infallible while recognizing that the specie's inherent defect?[5] I am not sure. But their attitudes might make sense if we were to explore the social regime under which men exist, coexist, and subsist.

Society could not exist on its own. The environment is part of the natural. Society is the most dangerous place for men to live. It is impossible for them to find peace and serenity in such a place. It is unlikely for men to secure their survival in such a space. Being in nature can be good for men; it offers them a different living experience.

---

[5] In *Crime and Nature*, I debate the origins of men. Also, see the book titled Natural Law: Morality and Obedience to learn more about this concept. To learn more about the concept of individual responsibility, consider reading this text.

Finding the Natural

In the natural world, a man does not need to prove himself worthy of life, liberty, and the ability to seek his own happiness. Every man has a tangible claim to life. Every man has a right to prosper. Every man shall advance in natural space. But the man shall do so on his own and for himself.

Men are exactly how their nature intended them to be. In nature, the man is likely to lose his way. In a social setting, it is likely that he will lose his beingness.

The common view is that nature is vast. The natural is unimportant. Nature is everywhere visible or anywhere imaginable by men. The environment is home to countless living entities. There, survival is guaranteed to no one. It is a *dog-eats-dog* place. The competition to live in the natural world can be fierce.

The man may find it hard to fit in within the natural space. He may not know where he belongs. He may not feel secure under his skin.

In the search for a better living experience, the man may waver from point to point. He may wander in futility through the space when he must carve himself a place to exist on his own and for his own sake. The man may wander through the environment in search of the perfect shelter to survive, which he may never find.

An everlasting search for natural space may lead to an artificial environment. But this place is antithetical to men. Here lies the dilemma of survival in men.

* * *

THE LIMITS OF LIFE IN SOCIETY

In a social setting, the life of a man can be agonizing. The person is expected to forego his essence. He shall renounce his natural leanings to fit into the space. These conditions are important for the person to be.

No other environment can be more lethal to human species than society. Within that space, the person shall arrive at a state of perfection, which is often illusory. But he shall do so as a strategy to uphold his nature within the artificial environment. The person shall lie to himself to preserve himself. He shall flirt with insanity as a precondition to remain sane.

Although men do not have it easy in the natural world, the artificial world can be a more dangerous for him. The person shall struggle relentlessly to overcome his obstacles. He shall deal with his troubles. Still, the man rarely succeeds in his search for being outside the reach of other men. As a result, the person is condemned to keep going. He would do so in perpetuity. He would be under the minions of other men for eternity.

In a social space, the person shall exert effort to preserve his worth. Except that it is a continuous battle. Still, the person shall push himself hard; he shall survive. The individual shall strive—strongly—to earn his place in the social space. He might do so more than expected.

Unlike the natural space, life in a social place can be artlessly demoralizing. The person might find it disheartening to preserve his existence. Although the individual should strive to outlast both society and nature, in a social hub, preserving one's life often becomes a struggle which the person would not—or could never—overcome.

In a social milieu, the individual has no recourse. He would not grumble when the social environment undermines his intrinsic worth. He finds himself in it. But he could not do away with it. The person must live in a social place. This painful certainty is beyond the will of a being.

In society, there is one way to be. There is no guarantee of survival; there is no certainty of existence. There, life is fleeting. Regardless, the person shall exist. There is no way for the individual to be other than by relying on fortuity.

To exist in a social milieu—or to be in the natural space—the person shall be attuned to the self. What

The Being in the World

this means is that the individual shall discover the ramifications of his beingness. He shall acquaint himself with the implications of the beingness of other living entities around him. The person shall also realize that nature is everywhere. He shall recognize that the natural always takes precedence. But the individual shall strive to find his nature. He shall place himself in the natural.

The person shall grapple with the reality—or the threat—that others pose to him in his environment. He shall strive to survive. He shall do so regardless of the limits, so imposed or so superposed, on him. But this is a state of being, which Men, as a species, seldom achieve. Few men know what it means to be, for they either lack the will to find it out or are incapable of such a feat.

Finding the Natural

5. We Are Ordinary Beings

There are no supermen in the world of men. Human beings are the same, at least to some extent. Although there are differences and nuances among human beings, these dissimilarities are so subtle that they are almost inconsequential to human beingness.

Our capacity to think has been a factor in our ability to make the cut in nature. There is an argument to be made about other living creatures that have been able to outlive this world as we have, although we do not communicate our survival skills to them. They have tapped into nature the same way that we, as humans, have done it. This reality suggests that they have a similar writ of the environment as we do.

There is the view that human beings rely on other entities to further their own existence. Everything we know about the world and most of what we know about ourselves in this environment comes from the knowledge we gained from other animals. The human body was not built up on its own.

We are Ordinary Beings

Everything that we are in the natural world comes from the beingness of another entity in the wilderness. What we eat is like what other animals eat. Where we live (our habitat) is like where other animals live or used to live. What we resemble is what other animals usually do. Our entire survival repertoire comes from the natural library. There is nothing new in the natural world that humanity invented or created from scratch. Our egotism is so great that we think we could conquer the world. This is illogical.

It is a fact that men have made substantial progress in the world. We made stunning leaps within the natural environment. Today we are thinking about going to Mars. We see this planet as a possible permanent hub for our kind. But I pity the foolishness of humankind.

Our hubris is so great that we become so vain. I begrudge our ability to see nothing when everything is right before our eyes. This does not mean that men could never cope on Mars. For our journey, we should also bring our dogs, our cats, our birds, our chickens, and our cattle. We should bring parts of the natural along the way because we are going to miss it.

Humans will be humans no matter what and wherever they go. We might find it difficult to be on Mars because we were not designed to be there. We could be nowhere other than planet earth; at least not in our current state of being.[6] We are ordinary humans. We belong solely to earth.

Despite our brittle nature, we might be exceptional here. Facets of the human experience separate us from other beings. No other mammals on the planet, at least known to us, could do what we can. Every hint suggests that we are unique. We also use our—supposed—uniqueness to alienate ourselves and others.

We run away from our natural state. What are we good for in the natural? What is the point of being? This is the basic question, which most thinkers have debated to no use.

* * *

ASSESSING HUMAN INVENTIONS

Human beings are the only primate known to men to have developed a language. We developed a means to communicate our thoughts on a tangible medium, such as a rock, a tree, or anywhere we can leave a mark. We developed writings; we developed

---

[6] I mean that the human body was not designed to be anywhere else other than planet earth. A new breed of human beings will change that reality. For now, we are condemned to be human. The humans of today are not extraordinary in the universe.

computers. We consider ourselves an advanced species. However, the nature of our progress within the natural topography remains a mystery; this is that way even to us.

After existing for millennia—on earth—we do not know why we are grounded in this environment, which we have grown accustomed to calling home. We are still searching for meaning. Despite our haughtiness, we are still clueless about ourselves.[7]

We know a lot about our history (as a species). It is irrefutable that we know a lot about the history of the planet we occupy. It is undeniable that we know where we came from. We know where we are in the universe (fairly); we have been to the Moon; we are striving for Mars; we have built a space for us in the space;[8] we have built wonders; we have made wonders. Even so, we do not impress the natural. From now on, we could not override the natural.

Nature always retorts against our haughtiness. It continuously comes back at us with vigor. The natural environment always undermines our hubris. It does so in full force and in the most degrading way.

---

[7] I refer to the environment as nature.

[8] I am referring to the International Space Station.

The natural space reminds us that we are inconsequential in the larger scheme of things.[9] This milieu sets apart the human species whenever it considers it necessary or whenever it chooses without warning. We are the slaves of our nature. This is so, no matter what we do. This is so regardless of what we think of ourselves.

As a species, we are hollow; we are trivial. We have no meaning beyond what we have given to ourselves. We are superfluous. We live to struggle; we struggle to live. But we have found a brim of meaning in our futile existence by making it even more precarious than it already is.

Unlike lions and tigers, which torment other species, we torment ourselves. What might explain why human beings make the living experience so unlivable for themselves? There is no proper way to explore this question without interjecting our own bias in the conversation.

Considering the epistemological drawbacks and the analytical shortfalls announced here, we must stress one facet of human beings. That side of the humanoid is captivating. Here, I am referring to the existence of a human being. I am also alluding to the

---

[9] What I am saying here is that nature always finds a way to undo what we did. Nature always finds a way to undermine our sense of superiority in the world. Nature always reminds us that we are just men, even though I tend to usurp ourselves as gods.

struggles humans face to uphold their existence in a world designed to consume that existence.

To what extent could a person's intrinsic ability to think improve his existence in the living space? This text discusses this idea further by examining a human thought.

* * *

UNDERSTANDING HUMANNESS

A human being is active 24 hours a day, seven days a week, four weeks a month, and twelve months a year. The human brain is restless. Once a human being is created, he is alive until the last molecule of the body breaks apart.[10]

What keeps us going? Why are we awake, even when we are asleep? Why are we always talking even when we are listening,[11] why are we always here and there, even when we are in one location? Why are we humans? A likely answer could come from our understanding of human consciousness.

---

[10] I am not making a pro-life or a pro-choice argument.

[11] The human mind is in a constant conversation with the self. A thought is a sublingual conversation with the self. That conversation never stops. If the being is alive, he/she is conversing with the self.

The Being in the World

A human being is always conscious, although the being is not always aware of that state of being (the human consciousness). Because of that state of always ON,[12] the person is in constant communication with the homestead and everything else within it. However, the living entity can be selective in the conversations he entertains with the surroundings.

Let us suppose that you are talking to John. During that conversation, several mini conversations are taking place, though not necessarily between you and John. You might ask John a simple question, such as what is your name? While John is answering that question, you might ask yourself other questions, which you could ask John next. You might do this subconsciously. You might do so as you listen to John's answer. While you do that, you might talk to yourself about other things, such as what John looks like; is he ugly? Is he smart? Is he lying? Is he talking too much?

You might ask yourself about other things as you interact with John. You might look at other people passing by. You might ask yourself something that is happening right now or something that might happen in the future. You might even reminisce about something that happened in the past.

---

[12] The human mind is and never OFF.

What is happening to your brain at that moment? A probable answer is that you are learning about yourself. You realize your conditions and the circumstances that others experience within the environment. You are multitasking. There is much more happening than a mere act of multi-thinking.

You are not engaged in several acts of thinking processes at once. You are merely engaged in a single act of thinking. The nature of the act is so complicated that even you—yourself—get lost in the process. But you shall keep yourself under control.

How human beings can keep themselves in check while they are thinking and talking at the same time. They drift—in and out—from one reality to another. To do so efficiently, the being shall refer to himself and in all places. The person keeps a constant conversational loop with the self, to the self, and about the self.

* * *

HUMAN THREE-DIMENSIONALITY

Let us revisit the conversation you had with John earlier. As you interacted with John, you kept checking with yourself along the way. At that point, you were not only engaged in the conversation, but you were also engaged in it. During the process, you were probing both yourself and the other person—John]. You may investigate anything else that entered your consciousness.

When you speak to John, you speak to yourself. As you listen to John, you listen to yourself. You might also listen to everything else in the environment. You are living the experience (or the conversation) at an intrinsic level. How is that feat possible? A likely answer is that you are indeed a multidimensional being.

A person—or a living entity—is divided into three entities. There is the—*you*—the *physical you* or the *being*. There is the—*possible you*—the *mental you* or the *abstract you*. Let us refer to that facet of the person as the *(self)*. There is the *(intrinsic you)*. I call this the—*you-within-you*—the *inner you,* or the—*you*—that overseas you. These entities are interlaced; they interact among themselves. They do so at the most fundamental level. They make up the *(you)*, which is seen physically. Here, a possible you, an intrinsic you, and you, as you are in the real world, form the three-dimensional you (*See* Figure 5.1).

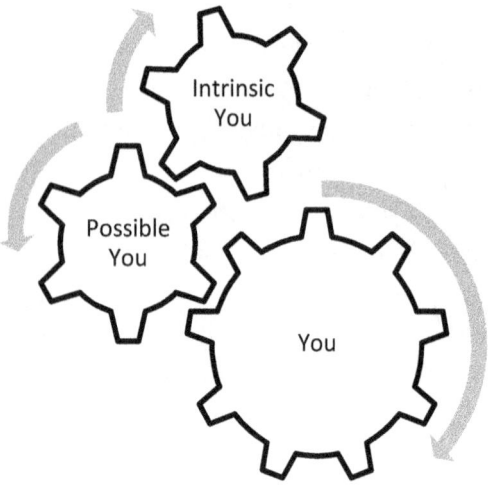

Figure 5.1 A Three-Dimensional You

There is a symbiosis between being and self. One needs the other to exist and vice versa. The *being* is constantly conversing with the *self*. The two entities do so automatically. Otherwise, they interact with each other in an automated way.

The being is always listening to the self. The self, by contrast, seldom considers the being. Even when the person is asleep, the being is engaging in a conversation with the self. That *private conversation* keeps the being in tune with the natural and all the entities that compose this milieu. That function keeps the being in the loop about both the self and any other entity that might interact with the self.

This factor tells the being about not only the self, but it does so also about the entities that exist within the environment.

The functionality to date exists only in three-dimensional entities. Not to mention that this reality affords the living entity an edge where it—he—lives. The entity is always one step ahead of any other entity (be they living or else), which could enter the consciousness of the living entity at any time.

The three-dimensionality of the human being is the essence of its/his beingness. Every living entity is three-dimensional. However, the extent to which every bearer of life is aware of their three-dimensionality is unclear. Only the living entity could answer this question. The entity could do so only for himself and for himself.

We are Ordinary Beings

SECTION III

INSANITY AND CONSCIOUSNESS

6. THE INSANITY LINE

The living entity hosts the being and the self, which lives in the self-within-the-self. These entities are constantly interacting. But the part of the entity, which is known as *the being,* could not afford to be too involved with the self. There is the danger of falling outside the accepted norms of human conversations. When the being converses with the self, he shall be cautious not to cross the insanity line.

A person should never be caught speaking (aloud) to the self, although the being is constantly conversing with thy self. The being should never be caught interacting with nature unacceptably, although the being is embedded in nature. By extension, the being is constantly interacting with the natural. Undeniably, whether the being—or the person—is aware of that reality is another question, the analysis of which is not our object here.

Being must be attuned to already settled social norms. Failure to do that could have profound consequences. A vital limit is worth considering. I describe it here as the *irrationality point*. The person should never violate this reality. When trying to suppress the nature of the individual, one also risks overlooking the reality of the individual.

At any rate, the person should never cross the insanity line or the irrationality point (so described in this case). Doing so could quash his beingness. The being might lose any sense of freedom. He might lose any privileges associated with his existence. In a social setting, the being is condemned to suppress his relationship with the natural. Whether consciously or otherwise, the being will undermine his own nature.

* * *

Denying the Self

The being is likely to deny the self, which often creates a problem for him. It is against the being to reject his own nature. It is inconceivable for him to reject the natural. It is naturally unfeasible for a being to do so by any means. The being has no tangible choice in a social setting. He shall overpower his nature; at least he shall try, persistently, to reach that goal.

The Being in the World

To live in a social space, the being shall abandon the self. He shall renounce his most intense biases. He shall deny himself a place to be himself. The being may live in an eternal conflict. He may not know how to be other than to be himself.

In a social space, the being shall be other than how his nature intended him to be. The problem is that the being could never concretize this aim. He shall deceive himself. He shall lie to the self about the extent to which he is in control of the self. Even if this doing so might be a perpetual failure.

The being could never be who he would like to be. He could never reach the state of being, which society expects from him. Although he may try, with effort, to be someone else, he will always fail. While on a conscious level, the being may try to be the person—or the entity—that others expect him to be, he will always revert to his intrinsic self.

In the end, the being would realize that he has no power over the self. He would never be sure of his dominion over the self, for the self—itself—is an elusive entity. The being would realize that he could not even discipline his own self. The being would find the self in a constant struggle to be someone other than who he is.

Denying yourself is a futile effort. All the same, efforts to overpower the self will always embolden the self, for the being would uncover the self in the most surprising manner. The being is seeking to tame a part of the self which he could never govern on his own. That part of the self can never be tamed.

While the being is tamable, the self is not. One reason that might explain that reality is that the self is not tangible that physical threats or other maniacal demonstrations could subdue. That situation may create a feeling of everlasting anxiety in the being.

The being is not sure how to be; he is no longer certain about where to be; he is confused about when to be. He is unclear on whom to be. The being is lost in the world.

* * *

A Lack of Certainty

The being is certain of nothing. He has no clue about his beingness within the immediacy. The being knows little about himself. He knows nothing about his being. The being knows nothing about the cosmos.

Despite his misgivings, the being knows that he exists. He knows that there are others around him. He can see them; he can touch them. He can see himself; he can sense himself. He knows that he is alive.

The Being in the World

The being is aware of the natural space. He can see the trees; he can see the rivers; he can see the world. He can sense other entities (both animated and inert). The being knows that these entities are aware of his existence. He is aware of their existence as well; at least, he does so at the subconscious level. Still, the being may lack certainty about everything, including the self.

The being could not claim—with confidence—that the sky is an illusion. He could not state that trees, ocean, landscape, or other beings are illusory. The being knows that they exist beyond any doubt.

The being also knows that he is not in control of himself. The individual understands that he is not in control of other living entities. The being realizes that he could not make sense of their existence; at least he could not do so faintly.

While the being might not be in control of the self overtly, he may sense his dominion over facets of the self. Secretly, the being is always aware of the self, though he could not grapple with the actuality of discovering the nature of that awareness. He could not intimate the self with the nature of the self at the most fundamental level.

To say it again, the being is aware of the self. At the most basic level, he is aware of everything in the natural. He might not be aware of that awareness. While the being is aware of the self, he might not be in tune with his own awareness of the self among other living creatures.

The being may be lost in his search for the self, which might reveal to him the nature of his own awareness. The self keeps eluding the being. Yet, the being keeps searching for the self. During that search, the being attaches a sense of self to the self. The being gives himself essence; he gives himself meaning, for, short of accomplishing this feat, the being would be lost in the world.

* * *

TALKING ABOUT THE SELF

As the being uncovers his ever-elusive self, he affords himself an essence. The being places the self in the world. He draws the line between the abstract and the physical self. The being separates the made-out sense of self from that of others. The being establishes his own identity.

What might be the value of a self-given essence? What makes a human being more valuable than a chicken, a lamb, or an ant? Are humans inherently superior? The answer is, to echo a previous assertion, no.

The common stipulation is that humans have traits that none of the formerly mentioned entities possess. I admit that humans appear unique. To avoid contradicting myself, the argument could be made that thinking affords not only human beings an edge in the natural. The assumption is that only humans can think.

How do we know that only humans can think? Well, we do not know that. We assume that this is the case. That assumption is based on our limited appreciation of nature and the entities in it, including ourselves.

The being might think that could also show his existence. This understanding is true regardless of the species or types of living entity. Every being in nature could think. Humans engage in such activities at a much deeper level. Human beings think at an introspective level. Why might that be the case? I am not sure.

If I were to speculate about human thinking abilities, I would say that humans enjoy a more marked sense of self. This is in part because the being is aware of the self within the natural, though he often has little knowledge of that self beyond the physical appearance of the self. I refer to this facet of the being as *the being*, which should be conflated with the living entity or the person.

* * *

TALKING ABOUT BEING

So far in the present dialogue, I have mentioned the term *being* recurrently. To be clear, the being, as referenced here, is only a part of the person or the living entity. Apart from that, the being is not the only entity that forms the person in the most tangible sense. The living entity, in its entirety, makes up the person, which includes diverse components and sub-entities, many of whom are not visible to the naked eye or perceptible by the common sensory apparatus.

If the living entity, which we could construe as a person, is alive, then it must have a being. However, the being is not the person in the most fundamental sense. The being is part of the entity, which could be construed as a person. That entity could be tangible or else it could be visible. Let me explain further.

Suppose that you are looking at a hairbrush. The entity that forms the hairbrush may include the physical brush and the functionality that the entity had been designed to perform. The hairbrush has two dimensions. The first dimension of the hairbrush is the object—or the item itself. The second dimension of the hairbrush comprises the functionality of the object. The hairbrush is only a hairbrush when it can brush hair. Otherwise, it is just an object, which may be used—or may not be used—to brush hairs.

The hairbrush is the entity that may or may not perform a specific task. The act of brushing is a capacity that is only relevant when the object or the entity is used as designed. For the entity described as a hairbrush to be a hairbrush in the most fundamental sense, it must exist—at first—as an object. Also, it must be able to function as a hairbrush. A hairbrush is that way only when it can be construed as an object, a tool, or an instrument that can brush hairs. That reality sets up the two-dimensionality of the hairbrush.

The same example applies to any living entity. Only similar entities are three-dimensional rather than two-dimensional. For instance, a person exists as a living entity. However, the entity comprises several other entities. The distinct entities of the person frame its dimensionality.

When I talk about a being in the context of an active entity, I am not referring to the self and vice versa. The self-in-and-of itself is not a living entity in its entirety. Instead, it is a part of the entity, which forms the person or the living entity as we know it.

The preceding statements may seem confusing. Bear with me. Let me clarify these ideas further.

* * *

LET'S TALK ABOUT BEINGNESS

The term beingness is not much different from the concept I note here as the *living entity*. As I sought to explain, the living entity is the person; it is the whole. That unit comprises three entities. They form the three-dimensionality of a living being or a living entity.

I could not imagine the living being from a distinct lens since the person or the being—or himself—is not the self. The being, at least as I describe it—or him—here, is an element of the global entity. That entity comprises many parts. In this context, I define the living entity as beingness.

When I say that, the being, I am referring to a facet of a living entity. When I say beingness, I mean a person, an animal, or any living entity. I could explore the term beingness from several angles. Let us say that the term beingness represents a man at a three-dimensional level.

Beingness, as a living entity, is animate. It is physical. That entity comprises both *flesh* and *blood*. We could describe beingness as a *man*. Any reference to the term *beingness* implies a person in his three-dimensional state.[13]

There is nothing extraordinary about human beingness. A person is supposed to be aware of his being. This involves a new reality. The person must establish a clear outline between his beingness, which is characterized by the being and the self. That awareness keeps the person alive. It keeps the living entity in constant conversation with other entities within the natural world. This is the essence of human beingness. Being in the world demands that the person understands his place in the cosmos. Preserving your beingness requires an understanding of the distinct parts of yourself.

The being is vulnerable in the world. But he is aware of that state of fragility. Self-awareness is the only buffer that keeps the self in control. The state of being (self-awareness) could be understood as the capacity of the being to ponder.

---

[13] I may also use the term being to refer to a person or a human being.

The Insanity Line

7. Human Consciousness

Human beings are always aware of themselves in the natural space. They are not always aware of that state of awareness. Only being aware of the self could help the being discover the self in the surroundings where he finds the self.

Human awareness results from their state of consciousness in nature. But there is more happening in the mind of the being. Even the being could get lost in his—own—realities. Let us consider the extent of human consciousness.

Suppose that we say that a person must be conscious as a condition to function normally in his environment. What are the requirements for consciousness? There are no straightforward answers. Beyond these bounds, we could consider two approaches.

Awareness is an element of consciousness itself. When you are aware of yourself and your surroundings, you are aware of yourself in your surroundings. You have a firm acumen of your identity. Does that mean that you always have a clear sense of the self (or even of others) within the environment? The answer is no.

We could take the former one step further. We could argue that human consciousness has many levels. A person would realize his consciousness at any point. But a man must know himself; he must know himself or the being.

The being would know that *being aware* of *the self* is the source of his consciousness. Yet that does not mean that the being is consciously aware of the self. Let us consider a person looking in a mirror. Would that person be able to see the self, or something related to the self? Would the person see some entity that is not necessarily the self? The possibilities are infinite.

Suppose that you decide to look at yourself in a mirror. Would you be able to see yourself as you are? Would you see yourself differently? Whom would you see in the mirror? Would it be you or someone else?

As long as you do not have a visual problem, you could see yourself or you could become cognizant of the fragments of yourself in that mirror. Is that all that is happening? Is there anything else going on during the process? What happened before you saw yourself? What is happening as you are seeing yourself? What will happen to your sense of self once you have seen yourself? Let us explore these ideas further.

* * *

WATCHING YOURSELF WATCHING YOU

Does the fact of looking at oneself in the mirror prove that one exists in one dimension or at a two-dimensional level? Is it a simple undertaking? The answer is no. There is more happening than the person on the other end of the mirror could allow the being to fathom. The figure below illustrates how the being watches the self watching him (*see* Figure 7.1)

Human Consciousness

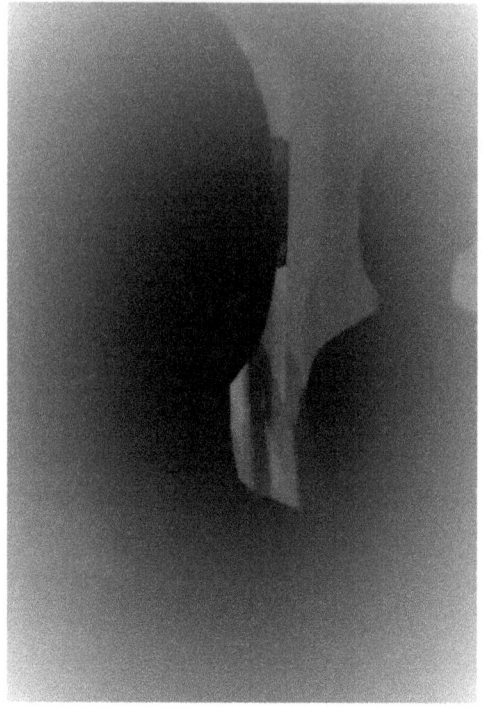

Figure 7.1: Watching yourself watching you

Before you could see yourself in the mirror, you must have had a preconceived idea of what you look like outside the mirror. You must already have a sense of self. The mirror is just a reflection of that self or the sense of that. Whether the self that you see in the mirror is the same self—who you are looking for—or is the self—which you already know—is not clear. But no being could be certain of his—own—self.

The *Cartesian approach* to self-discovery suggests that the being is constantly searching for the self. The being is never certain of the self. The being is in an everlasting state of doubt. René Descartes would say that a state of doubt makes one aware of oneself. That awareness gives essence to the being.

I do not challenge the *Cartesian approach* to self-discovery; at least, I do not do so here. I must concede that a state of doubt alone would not confirm yourself. What it might do is that it might allow the self the capacity to recognize itself within the self.

For the being to doubt, he shall be able to compare the self with something other than thyself. Through that comparison, the being might either confirm or reject his apprehensions about the self. The *Cartesian mode* of studying the being is incomplete.

Something else is taking place in the being. It may induce the being to doubt the self. The being could not doubt the unknown. If the being is going to doubt the self, the being must already have known the self.

To go back to our mirror example; the being may see the self. Otherwise, he may envisage the self from a three-dimensional angle. This is the essence of being in the world.

SEARCHING FOR YOURSELF

Human beings are always searching for their own look. Why do we do so? What could explain why we often seek ourselves in our own look? A lack of certainty about yourself is the reason we are constantly searching for it.

The self is not always obvious to the being. Recall that the human entity exists in a three-dimensional state. But the being is aware of only two dimensions of the self. One facet of the person always escapes him. That side of the self makes the self, which the person is constantly searching, elusive, even to the self.

As the person searches for himself, he meanders back and forth between who he is and who he hopes to be. The line that separates the two entities is a representation of the real self, which will never be tangible to a point of capture. The elusive nature of the self may condition human existence in the most fundamental sense. That everlasting search makes the self, in a manner of speaking, elusive—in and of itself—to a point where the pursuit of the self never ends. That pursuit, to underline it, is the essence of human survival.

The way to appreciate the hitherto reality is by examining when a person is looking in a mirror. A state of consciousness would reveal to the person the absence of the self, which would induce a search, though subconsciously, for the self. But it is a paradox; otherwise, it leads to a dead end. That search would never be completed, for the self keeps alluding to the one trying to place the self.

To elucidate the aforementioned assertion further, let us point out that when a person looks in a mirror, he always searches for his own look. The person looking in the mirror is always looking for the eyes (or the look) of the other person in the mirror. The person does that instinctively. Omitting other circumstances, he does so inasmuch to be certain that he is looking at the right person or he is gazing at the right entity. This is a way to confirm preconceived expectations about the self.

The looker must be sure that he has found the person whom he has been looking for in the mirror. The look (the eyes) of the entity in the mirror would either confirm or reject the expectations of the person who is gazing at the mirror. This back and forth between the person looking at the mirror and the person being looked on sets up a two-dimensional panorama, which either confirms the look or rejects it. For most people, this is where the experience ends. Setting this reality aside, there is more to the self than might be readily obvious.

* * *

The Revelation About the Self

A look reveals nothing about the person breeding it. As the individual seeks the self, he would never find it. At some point, he may abandon the search; he may contend with the self of having glimpsed the self, which, in and of itself, may reveal nothing novel about the self. This is the misfortune of human consciousness.

The second a person is aware of the self. But he may lose that sense of self. A person could never be certain of the self, for the self keeps eluding him. The person is caught in a constant loop of finding and losing the self. Every time the person sees the self, he wonders whether this is the true self. The self keeps reminding the person who he should be this way or that way.

A third dimension is worth considering as we progress in this discussion. That dimension could be understood as the entity within the self, which allows the person the capacity to compare the known self with the expected self. Through the look, the person probes whether he is looking at the right entity. The look is just a confirmation of the knowledge the person already holds about the self or the entity he is looking at in the mirror. A look is only part of the self-discovery process.

A look in a mirror is also a familiar sight. You already know yourself—at least physically. You must have known yourself introspectively—or even psychologically—to identify the self during a routine look of the self or the body, which serves as a vessel for the self.

The look is a confirmation of known biases about the self. It is a confirmation of information which the person had (or recently gathered) about the (supposed) self. The look, in and of itself, and to say it again, reveals little—or nothing—about the self or the person starting the look.

When you look at yourself in the mirror, you already know where certain marks are on your body. You already know where the physical shapes or other tangible features are throughout your body. You know who you are; you know what you look like. You know your particularities. You know what specific traits of your body look like.

As you assess yourself, you gauge your own assessment of the self. What you look like as a person could be irrelevant as long as your actual physical traits match your established sense of self.

You could be as ugly as they come. So long as you believe that you are pretty, you would never see ugliness in you. The opposite is also true.

You could be as pretty or as handsome as they come. However, so long as you believe that you are ugly, you would never see the beauty in you. You may recognize your physical features with just a glance. Yet, that would not undermine the subjective nature of your interpretation of yourself.

* * *

REJECTING THE SELF

A look in a mirror is never definite. The more you gaze at yourself in a glass, the more likely you would doubt the self that you see or the self you may sense. The more likely you might reject the self.

As you are watching yourself in the mirror, something interesting is also happening, though you may not be aware of it. Either you would confirm your—own—expectations about yourself or you would be intrigued by what you see. You might become curious about any distinctive feature of yourself. You might get distracted by yourself. You might think about your own appearance. You might even reject your physical appearance by claiming that something is wrong with the mirror.

In the end, you might even reject your own being, as it might not suit your expectations. This state of affairs happens when people do not notice discolorations on this skin. The same could happen when people did not notice changes in their physical body because of aging or other effects related to human being.

As you look at yourself, you might overlook yourself. You might look for a specific location on yourself. Thus, you might only see yourself subconsciously.

Suppose that when you are trying on a new outfit (a shirt, a pair of pants, or a dress) or a new pair of shoes, you might not look at your whole body. As you try on the apparel, your eyes may be drawn to your upper areas. At the end of the look, you must look at yourself in the eyes. Failure to do so could lead to an incomplete look.

Human Consciousness

Section V

Introspection and Awareness

8. An Incomplete Look

What is an *incomplete look*? We could parallel this question from several angles. But let us take a practical approach.

An incomplete look or *IL* is failing to decipher a clear sense of an item or an entity after a look. If I were to look at a sight, be it in movement or in stationery, I would not look at that sight. I may know little or nothing about that sight, for my look at it was incomplete.

Most of what we look at during a regular gaze is incomplete. We may look at an item or an entity. Whether we saw it is a different question. Yet we do not see the item or the entity. We must know the look.

We do not always make an awareness of that activity. The item (or the entity) does not always enter our consciousness.

Every look is three-dimensional. Whether you are looking at the self or someone else, every look must go through a process of (1) Gazing, (2) Assessing, and (3) Synthesizing. An incomplete look would occur whenever you failed to take the following steps. The figure below illustrates the looking process (*see* Figure 8.1).

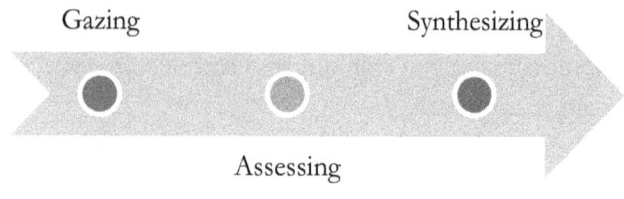

Figure 8.1: The Looking Process

When a look is incomplete, the looker must look again. Until the process is completed, the looker might not look at anything else. The brain might refuse to process any added information, which might be inaccurate. The brain would reject any uncompleted data about the entity that is also under scrutiny during a look.

When I speak of gazing, I am referring to the act of looking. The eyes of a person are locked into a particular entity. That entity could be in a fixed state;

it might be stationary. Otherwise, it might be in motion.

Assessing is the process by which the looker is trying to make sense of the information that he is gathering about the entity at which he is gazing. The assessment is a state where the looker compares what he knows about the entity in which he is gazing at in time. There, the looker makes a subjective appreciation of the entity under scrutiny.

The synthesizing process is more sophisticated. The looker already gathered the information *(the gaze)*. He already compared that information with already known data *(assessing)*. The looker may try to be as objective as he can in his analysis of the entity under scrutiny. He must confirm—or he must reject—the already gathered data. He must do the same for the already assessed (not processed yet) information. This is where the looker can doubt the self.

* * *

THE EFFECTS OF LOOKING AROUND

Let us say that Patrick (a 19-year-old male) enjoys going to the mall in the evenings to admire the beauty of the other sex. He usually picks a spot

An Incomplete Look

where he could see all the women entering or leaving the mall. Now, being able to see both the entrance and exit of everyone in and out of the mall is essential for Patrick. This is the only way that the young man could enjoy this activity to its fullest.

For every person of interest who passes in front of Patrick, he must perform the three steps mentioned earlier. First, Patrick must gaze. Then, he must assess. In the end, Patrick must synthesize the person from head to toe. To do so, Patrick must have a look at every person of interest. How would this process occur?

Patrick must begin and complete the look himself. To start the look, the young man must look at the frontal areas of the person, which may include the face, arms, upper body, and legs. Patrick must look at the entire body of the entity under scrutiny. At this point in the activity, the young man may not be aware of that knowledge. He may be too busy collecting the data; he may be too busy processing the information he gathered about the targeted person or the entity in question.

Patrick must look at the person's back areas. They may include the back of the head (hairstyle), arms, posterior, and legs. Once all the needed information had been gathered, Patrick could confirm—or he could reject—any preconceived notions about the person.

The Being in the World

Patrick might think that the person is an exquisite beauty. He might also think that the person is a rare specimen of ugliness (la personne est d'une laideur incomparable et repoussante). Patrick has not synthesized the information gathered so far. What would give Patrick the framework that would allow him to gauge the person who is passing by? The answer is the environment.

Patrick could refer to known information about humans to assess one person exhaustively. This might be the best way for Patrick to gauge them. Otherwise, what the young man knows about one person could be based on what he has learned about others in the past. The collected information could be based on what the collectivity has determined about human beingness.[14] Somewhere along the way, Patrick must make his own determination (or the illusion of that) about the person who he is gazing.[15]

Only when Patrick has completed the gaze, the assessment, and making up his preconceived notions could we say that the look is complete. Patrick would complete the look as soon as he was finished

---

[14] By using collectivity, I am referring to society itself.

[15] There is a back and forth between subjectivity and objectivity. Patrick must reconcile what he thinks about the person and what he knows about the person. The inability to do so would lead to an incomplete look.

collecting essential information about the person. The young man would do so as soon as he finished processing that information according to his preconceived notions about the entity under scrutiny. The looker must look at both the front and the back of the person he is looking at. Otherwise, the look would be incomplete.

A unique process takes place with moving entities, as opposed to entities that are fixed. In the earlier example, Patrick was gazing at moving entities. But when one looks at oneself in the mirror, the entity is not necessarily in motion. Anyhow, the three-dimensional process must occur.

* * *

A Three-Step Process

When you look at yourself in the mirror, the three steps mentioned above must occur as well. First, you must look at yourself. You must look at or towards your own eyes. Second, you must assess the information collected. Third, you synthesize that knowledge with your preconceived notions about yourself (*see* Figure 7.1).

The look is complete once you have been able to accept or reject the information you gathered about yourself. Therefore, doubt alone could not confirm you. A doubt results from a series of events, which must precede the self.

The being could not doubt the self unless the being already knew the self. The problem is that the being is seldom aware of the self. True, sometimes the being might have a good sense of self. But if that were to be the case, at which point could the being and the self-self be considered two separate entities?

Both the being and the self are always apart. They are never the same. These entities must work in tandem. The being needs the self. The self is useless without a being as a point of reference.

The being does not experience what the self—itself—lived through. They are not the same. There is a significant difference between being in pain and imagining what it would be like to be in pain.

Under any circumstances, the being could communicate a sense of pain to itself. Either way, the self could not do the same for the being. Here, I could not imagine being in such a pain. There is a clear divide between the two experiences.

The self could create a sense of pain in the being by making the being expect an actual sense of pain. The being would feel pain, even though it might not be the actual pain. This experience might be enough to affect the state of the being.

The self could deceive the being into being a certain way, which the being might not have been on his own. The self could manipulate the being. The self could induce a sense of fear in the being because there are reasons in the environment, which may prompt the being to react to a particular stimulus. Being could create a sense of peace and tranquility when there might be enough reasons to be scared. Does that mean that the being enjoys full control over the self? The answer is no.

* * *

FREEDOM AND EXISTENTIALISM

Existentialist theorists would argue that humans are free. But existentialists seldom admit a fact about human freedom. Simply put, freedom is not available in the real world. The being only enjoys a sense of being free and not actual freedom.

On the face of the relation, the being outwardly enjoys with the self, and he seems free to engage the self. All the same, the self seems free to engage the being. This freedom (if we could call it that) is only illusory. It is often imagined, created, and experienced at an introspective level.

The Being in the World

The being lives in the real world. The self—a part of the person—wonders back and forth between the real and the surreal. It is not always clear when the self is in either state. The being could be lost in the biases of the self. The self could lead to the premature extinction of the being, notably by asserting itself unnecessarily.

Both the being and the self are not alone. For that reason, human beingness comprises three entities. That is why humans are three-dimensional beings.

Discovering the self—or the mechanism of discovering others—pegs the being to take three steps. The outcome of the discovery process is the synthesis of both known information and newly picked up data about the self. Also, that synthesis could only be conducted by another entity. I refer to this entity as the self-within-the-self.

An Incomplete Look

9. THE SELF IN A MIRROR

When you look in the mirror, you can see yourself from a two-dimensional standpoint (*see* Figure 9.1). That self, in some ways, forms a reflection of the being. The self could be anything the being wants it to be. The self could manipulate the being to become anything it might want it to be. Here, the man in the mirror is looking at the self as the self is gazing at the man in the mirror.

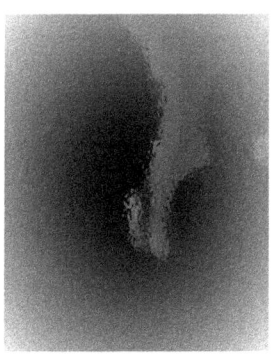

Figure 9.1: The Man in the Mirror

The Self in a Mirror

Most people are aware of their physical characteristics. When you look in the mirror, you gloss over your body. Surely, you are not aware of what you see as you look at yourself. However, you always know your physical self. If not, you always have that sense.

Sometimes you might focus solely on some specific areas of your body. In such cases, you might realize the act of looking at yourself. As expected, this does not mean that you are aware of yourself intrinsically. It means that you are aware of certain aspects of yourself or your body. You would examine facets of yourself that might not be plain to others.

The man in the mirror might not have power over the man in front of the mirror. The man standing in front of the mirror could deceive the man in the mirror. He could do so no matter what his circumstances might be. The man watching the man acting on the man in the mirror controls the man in front of the mirror and the man in the mirror.

As you look in the mirror, you are also *watching yourself*. Even if you do not always make out that interaction; at least, not in real time. You are not ineluctably aware of your awareness at the time you are aware of yourself.

As you realize yourself when you become aware of the self (that is, yourself), that awareness may vanish away. You may lose focus; you may lose any sense of awareness. It is as if you had awakened from a dream or a moment. You must redirect yourself to yourself or the entity on which you were originally focused. You must adjust to yourself.

Who does that readjustment? You do it on your own. Of course, you are not necessarily aware of it.

Let us revisit the conversation you had with John in the earlier chapter (Chapter 5) to make sense of it all. Under any circumstances, you must keep reminding yourself that John is talking to you. This is how you keep that conversation going, even when you may not have heard half of what John said to you.

You are not always aware of yourself within the arena where you live. You may see yourself as part of the natural setting. But when you have a sense of awareness of the environment, only then would you realize the extent of that place.

On a subconscious level, you do not always distinguish yourself from a tree. You do not always see a difference between yourself and anything else within the environment unless a particular entity enters your consciousness at any point. Only then would you realize that entity. Let us consider another example, which might help clarify that assertion further.

The Self in a Mirror

* * *

HUMAN AWARENESS

Suppose that you are walking the streets? What would you see? In most modern cities, the streets are often busy. There are cars passing by; there are people walking by; there are shops; there are obstacles on the way. There might be sidewalks; there might be decorative trees; there might be benches; there might be merchants or other entities. You must know all these items; otherwise, you must be attuned to all these entities as you walk by them.

As you walk the streets, you are not always aware of the entities within the environment. You are not always aware of the things that are on your way as you pass by. Of course, there are noteworthy exceptions. There are conditions that might distract you from your reality, at least in certain situations.

You could realize certain items or situations, notably those that have caught your attention in some way or another or entered your consciousness. You may realize that you are aware of these items.

If you became distracted and ignored the sign that says *do not walk*, you might be hit by a car. You may lose your feet and miss your steps while walking. You might bump into someone; else you might get in trouble with something. You might even trip and fall to the ground. This is what might happen if you cannot be aware of your awareness at any moment during your existence.

The observed reality does not mean that you did not see the car. It does not mean that you missed the sign that warned you not to cross the street. It does not mean that you did not see the person coming towards you. It does not mean that you overlooked the bench or the lamppost that had been buried on the grounds for many years. Only you got distracted. As a result, you did not have the time to alert yourself to the danger ahead.

The being is not always aware of the self. The person is not always aware of his awareness. People are not aware of their awareness. Human beings are not always aware of their beingness. This makes their being precarious both in society and within the natural. That reality could be dangerous to the being of a person.

* * *

THE EXTENT OF SELF-AWARENESS

Based on what we have discussed so far, could we say with the utmost certainty that human beings are always aware of themselves in their environment?

The Self in a Mirror

This is not necessarily the case. What does that mean in practical terms?

Let me put it this way; is it so that not being aware of yourself could lead to premature death? The answer is yes.

Being aware of the self is the best way for the being to preserve his beingness. The world is a noisy place. The being is always overwhelmed by outside stimuli; the mind is constantly distracted. Being aware of yourself is not always possible. Preserving the self is not always possible.

The being (for example, the human body) is in a constant conversation with nature and the self. As nature speaks to the being, the self—in this case—assesses that information and dictates to the being what to do according to what is doable. Most of what a being does, he does without realizing it.

As I type these words on these pages, I am assessing whether they are the right words to use. I am discussing with myself whether I should say more. Whether I speak aloud to myself, whether I whisper, whether I ponder (I think), or whether I reflect subliminally or else, I am conversing with the self. In any manner workable or in any form imaginable by me, I am conversing with both nature and self—myself.

On an intrinsic level, I am communicating with both the natural and myself. I am performing this function simultaneously. That conversation is so settled that I am not always aware that it is happening.

Some realities that my being might experience might also want me to notice the situations I am experiencing. This idea might not apply to my survival. They might not help me preserve my being in the end.

I might want to suppress the conversation I am having with myself. I might also want to ignore that conversation. When I am aware of that *tête-à-tête*, I might suppress it. I might ignore it to a point of exasperation. Of course, my body might force me to note that conversation.

* * *

IGNORING MY NATURE

It can be impossible to ignore one's nature. As I am typing these words, for instance, my body is asking for a bathroom break. Because I am so entrenched in the ideas that I am putting in the document, I keep postponing the conversation. Yes, my body makes me aware of that unpleasant reality that is boiling within me. I am also determined to ignore that conversation.

The Self in a Mirror

While I may find my nature too intrusive, I may have no choice but to respond to its demands. At some point, I will have to respond to the conversation that my body wants to have with me. No matter what I do, I could not ignore my nature. I will have to respond appropriately to the demands of my body at the right time.

My being is based on whether I am alive. The best way to find out whether someone is alive is not always clear. There is no universal way to gauge being.

There are ways to tell whether someone is alive. One way to tell whether someone is alive is by seeing him breathing. The person who is breathing is not always aware that this is reality happening. Most people do not know that they are alive. Being alive differs from having knowledge of that likelihood or that state of fact.

Human beings do not spend their lives making sure they are alive. Human beings do not perceive their *livingness* as being reduced to a simple exercise of breathing. We often overlook (or we often undervalued) activities which could show our being. We often expose our beingness without our awareness. There lies the danger of being.

Section V

Dimensionality and Awareness

10. A THREE-DIMENSIONAL ENTITY

Based on what we have discussed in the preceding chapters, it could be said that *beingness* is an amalgam of entities. It is a compilation of three entities. These entities interact with the natural in their own way. Their interaction with the world is the beingness.

The beingness is an elusive entity. It is a representation of the person in the three dimensions outlined in previous chapters. The being comprises a *being,* a *self,* and a *self-within-the-self.* That is the reason the being could be understood from a three-dimensional angle. The figure below sketches the nature of the being when examined from a three-dimensional lens.

We could imagine human beingness as a big box. Inside that box, there are two other boxes. Together, they form the beingness. The little box is an element of another box; only that box is bigger. That element

A Three-Dimensional Entity

is the pillar of a bigger box, which is not visible. This box is also camouflaged by two other boxes, as explained below (see Figure 10.1).

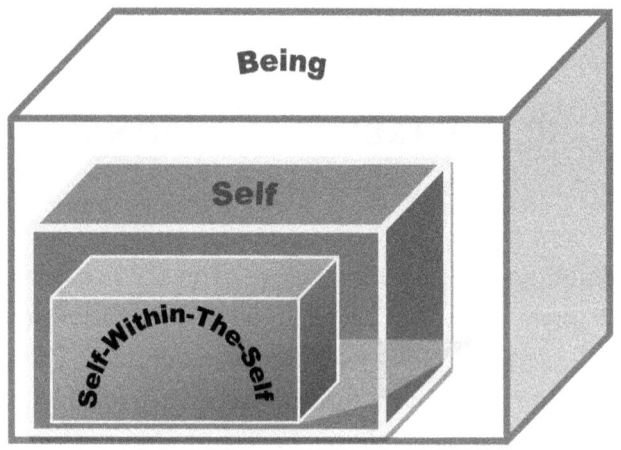

Figure 10.1: A Three-dimensional entity

* * *

THE BEING

Of the three entities mentioned earlier, one is inherently tangible. This entity comprises flesh and bones. It always experiences the physical reality of the person in the present or at the moment. We could refer to this entity as the *being*.

The Being in the World

The being, as an entity, can be seen; he can be touched; he can be heard; he can be felt; he can be experienced not only by the self but also by other beings. The *being* is a vessel that carries the other two entities. The being is the tangible—or the material—representation of the living entity.

The being is the physical entity that interacts with the world. It feels pain; it displays joy; it shares other kinds of emotions; it experiences the world for what it is. Destroying the being, we could say, would be the extinction of the *self* and the *self-within-the-self*.

The *being* is a host entity. The being is the person whom you can see and touch. However, the being is not the *self*.

※ ＊ ＊

THE SELF

Another entity worth mentioning in this analysis is the self. This unit experiences existence both in the present and in the past. It is elusive. It is possible to see; it is easy to feel; it is easy to touch; it is not an impossibility to experience, notably by other beings. This unit does not enjoy invisibility, though it could

A Three-Dimensional Entity

be hidden or even patently subtle,[16] but it is part of the core of the being.

The *self keeps* the being relevant. Without self, the being is useless and would not *be* for a long time. The *being* cannot be without the self. The *self*, as an exogenous entity, affords the person identity and purpose.

The being exists so long as the *self l*earns to communicate with the *being*. There is a symbiotic relationship between the two. The former needs the latter tangentially to flourish.

The *self* is the essence of the being. The *being* is the pillar on which the *self* exists. The *being* is always asserting the *self*. The *self* is constantly noticing the *being*.

Let us retrace the mirror example mentioned earlier. In this scenario, we could say that the *being* is asserting the *self* through looking. The *self-recognizes* the *being* by assessing the look.

Suppose that you look at yourself in a mirror. Who do you think you would see? For most people, the answer is simple. They might tell you that a look in a mirror would reveal a reflection of themselves. When you look in a mirror, you would see *yourself*. You would see *you*.

---

[16] It could be visible through the being.

Is it possible that you would not see *you* per se? If that were to be the case, what would you see? What you might see in the mirror could be *yourself;* you-yourself as an entity, which would not cardinally be *you* in the most material way (or in the most tangible sense) of the word *you*. It would be a representation of the real *you*. Only, it would not be the—*you*—whom you think is in the flesh and bones.

You, as a *being,* would be part of—*yourself*—which is a discrete entity in and of itself. The *self* is much bigger than the figure, the *you* that you see in the mirror. The *self* is part of your *beingness*. It is not your beingness in and of itself.

* * *

THE SELF-WITHIN-THE-SELF

The third entity, which I identify in this concept, is *self-within-the-self*. I will explore this entity in depth in the following subsection. For now, let us say that the *self-within-the-self* experiences the world at an introspective level. What does that mean intrinsically? Let us explore further.

For starters, this entity expects the terrain. It interacts with the world at a different level. The self-within-the-self is the overseer of both the self and

A Three-Dimensional Entity

the being. This entity experiences the reality of both the being and the self in the present, the past, and the future.

The self-within-the-self has a complex role in keeping the person alive. It is in constant communication with the environment. It tells the being about the environment. It incites the being to preserve beingness. This is the essence of the being.

This entity is in tune with the milieu more than the *being* could fathom. This is the buffer between the real and the surreal. This is the line between a dream and a reality. It draws a wedge between the mind, the soul, and the body.

11. Who Is (Truly) in the Mirror?

As you look in a mirror, there are three facets of yourself, which (as a whole) make up your beingness. There is the *being,* the *self,* and the *self within the self.* The latter entity is the core of your beingness. It is the foundation of your being. Without it, you have no self. Then again, you depend on yourself. Without a *self,* your existence might go extinct.

The *self-within-the-self* guides the *self.* Both the being and the self must cohabit on this pillar. This entity gauges the *self*, while the self must gauge the being. The *self-within-the-self* keeps it all together.

The *self-within-the-self* is difficult to gauge from within or from the inside. You do not know the *self-within-the-self.* Except that it knows you. The *self-within-the-self* is never visible to other beings. This entity is the core of your beingness.

This entity is in constant communication with the world; it does so both inside and outside. It knows the landscape more than the environment will reveal itself to you. It tells you about the events occurring close by that might escape the vigilance of both the being and the self. Some people refer to that entity as instinct or intuition. It is the essence of your being.

The term *Preserving Your Beingness* (*see* the publication of the same title)[17] does not refer only to the *being*, the *self*, or the *self-within-the-self*. The concept refers to all three entities. No doubt, it might be difficult, if not impossible to preserve the *self-within-the-self*. The nature of this entity includes invisibility and elusiveness.[18] How do you tap into that part of your beingness? The answer is philosophy.

By appealing to the *self-within-the-self*, you could have an edge in your environment. This advantage would give you the ability to prolong your survival. You can only reach out to this entity by being aware of your environment. But you must do so at the most intrinsic level.

---

[17] Preserving Your Beingness

[18] This entity functions with the realm of your subconsciousness. It is a part of your beingness.

* * *

ASSESSING THE CONCEPT OF BEINGNESS

The beingness comprises three elements. They include the *being,* the—self—and the—*self-within-the-self.* The living entity must preserve all three facets of the self as it is to be. Let us explore these concepts further.

Before we go further in this analysis, let me say that preserving one's being is more complicated than you may think. By no means is this idea inconceivable; it is attainable in the genuine sense of the term. I have lived by these sets of rules for a good portion of my life. I have faced tough situations. But I have only been able to live another day because of my intrinsic ability to listen to myself. I have endured because of my tendency to follow my instincts at all corners of my existence.

My estimation of the being is not that odd. Preserving oneself is an intrinsic human impulse. Human beings are born to be. Every person must preserve themselves. The individual must do so all the time, if not always.

When considering that we are likely to live in a social space, it is also important to note that we are likely to let go of ourselves. We are prone to overlooking the danger of being. We underestimate the risk that geography poses to yourself.

We expose ourselves to danger unnecessarily. It is necessary to highlight the precocity of the social environment. But that reality might be equated as a chimerical effort. Even if there is a need to assimilate how society could be lethal for the being. The being—or the person—must—constantly—be aware of the self. That is the reason society could be as lethal as the jungle for the being. The person must incorporate himself into the artificial environment, while considering his vulnerabilities within that environment.

Revealing oneself to a leopard, a snake, a tiger, or other pathogens in the natural differs from revealing the self to the dangers of society. Unlike the jungle, society has no cure to help the person mitigate lethal situations. The being could not evade a leopard the same way he might seek to evade the police or other entities. Unless excluded, the result of face-to-face interaction could be similar (if not worst) in a social setting.

The being could be victimized. The being could be deprived of his beingness amid the struggle to find means to survive. Thus, there is always a reason to preserve the self in a social setting.

Humans have a natural impulse to rise to the occasion to face the challenges of their environment.

People know instinctively how to do the same. The human species has survived for thousands of years. From here, the being picked up his surviving skills from the natural milieu itself. This expertness occurs through a constant stream of communication between the being and the natural.

* * *

COMMUNICATING WITH NATURE

How does nature communicate survival skills to the being? Nature is the primary teacher of human existence. The being may determine these skills based on the clues that nature gives him here and there. The being learns to live by paying close attention to the natural world. It would be the environment where the person lives.

A being who is in tune with his nature has a greater chance of survival in the natural world. The set of skills that a being receives from nature is not useful only alone. Such skills could be useful to being in a social environment as well.

The being must know himself within the environment where he lives. The being must understand that he is fragmented into three parts that are quintessential for his long-term survival.

The being must recognize the self and the *self-within-the-self*. The being must be in touch with the real world. From this perspective, it is always important to look at the being. The figure below illustrates the nature of beingness. (*See* Figure 11.1).

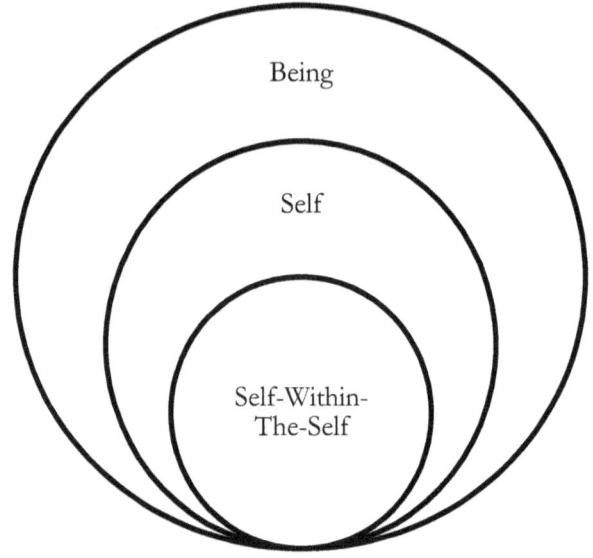

Figure 11.1: The Beingness

To echo a previous assertion, the *being* (as an entity) experiences the natural landscape directly and as it is presented to him. The *self* (as an entity), in contrast, assesses what the *being* experiences at any given point. In that capacity, the self must dictate the *being* what course of action might be more suitable in a particular situation. Let us explore this idea through a practical lens. This reality allows the self to control the self, at least to the extent that the self would allow itself to be tamed by *the-self-within-the-self*.

Who is (Truly) in the Mirror

12. CONTROLLING THE SELF

Suppose that Cledanor is at home; he is taking a nap. Suddenly, a fire broke out in a room near his bed. For a while, Cledanor was unaware of the fire, for he was in a deep sleep. At some point, the young man realized that there was a fire in the house. He suddenly woke up. Which part of Cledanor first noticed the fire? What led Cledanor to wake up?

A probable answer is that both Cledanor, the *being* (or the physical entity) and Cledanor himself or the *self* (the half-abstract entity and half-physical entity) had been aware of the fire at the specific moment before he awoke. It took the *self-within-the-self* to provoke a chain of reactions, which finally woke Cledanor up. Until that intervention, the young man was at the mercy of the environment. Cledanor had to be aware of both the *self* and his *being* as a single mechanism. Doing so would enable the young man to preserve his beingness.

Controlling the Self

Before Cledanor awoke, his body (his physical being) was aware of the fire. Under the circumstances, the young man himself (*the self*) was not aware of that experience. As soon as Cledanor realizes the fire, he would dictate the body what to do. The young man would seek the nearest exit. He would have to effort his best to preserve his beingness, which would include all three entities (the *being,* the *self,* and the *self-within-the-self*).

Let us decipher the *self-within-the-self* a little further. This entity sees the self, as the—*self*—witnesses the *being* in the sublunary world. There is constant communication between the *self* and the *self within the self.* That back and forth is what allows the *being* the capacity to uncover the world for what it is and not necessarily what it looks like superficially. It would not be based on what or how the environment might want the *being* to sense it.

Both the *self* and the *self-within-the-self* are in constant interactions with the environment. They tell the being about why and how he should be. This communication often forces the being to pick up important knowledge and skills, which might help him (the being himself) to develop the capacity to make sense of the milieu. This might also help him find the means to suffer in it.

As a precondition to be in the environment, the *being* must catch the drift of whom, what, why, when, and where he should be. Philosophy is the only introspective tool, which affords the being the means to stay in touch with the self and other entities in a milieu where he lives. That is why philosophizing is the most important side of being in the world. It is the quintessence of life itself.

* * *

THE PILLAR OF HUMAN EXISTENCE

Philosophy could help the person discover a map of the world. That discovery would enable the being the ability to achieve a state of inner peace within the social environment where he lives. The being needs to philosophize. That is how he could exist beyond providence.

As the being pondered, he would pick up a good sense of the world and the entities in it. That knowledge would enable the ability to brew a means to hold out continually in that environment. This is the essence of being natural. The figure below illustrates the mechanism of the cogito (*see* Figure 12.1). I refer to this reality as the *cogito* or philosophizing. Let us explore this notion in greater detail.

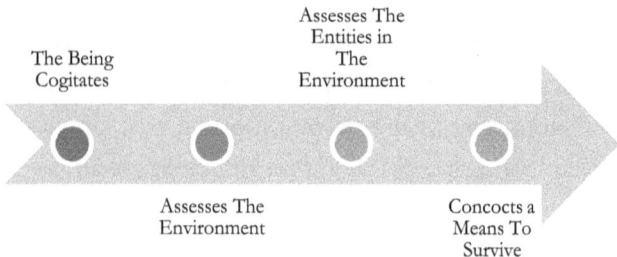

Figure 12.1: The Philosophizing Process

Pondering alone might not be enough to allow a man to thrive in this world. The being shall have a sense of the gathered information beyond the mere recognition of the collected data. In the same vein, the being shall combine the information gathered. He shall do so for the same purpose.

As a condition to meet that expectation, the being shall reflect about the self and the entities that interact with that self. The being shall know his role in the environment. I call this process *philosophizing* or the philosophizing process.

The being engages in thinking only so he could be despite of any eventuality. He does so as a strategy to be in the cosmos. This is the most effective way to philosophize. This is also the prime point of being in nature.

There is a process to being. The process starts with the act of thinking. The being shall discover the self in the environment. Thinking affords the being the means to find the self.

As the being engages with the self, he realizes thyself. That awareness allows the being to make sense of the self in the environment. As the being makes sense of the self, he may gauge the self. That act, in and of itself, may cause the self to reflect on the self. The person is philosophizing. The figure below illustrates how to being engages in the cogito (*see* Figure 12.2).

Controlling the Self

- The being engages the self
- The being becomes aware of the self
- The being makes sense of the self
- The being gauges the self
- The being reflects on the self
- The being cogitates

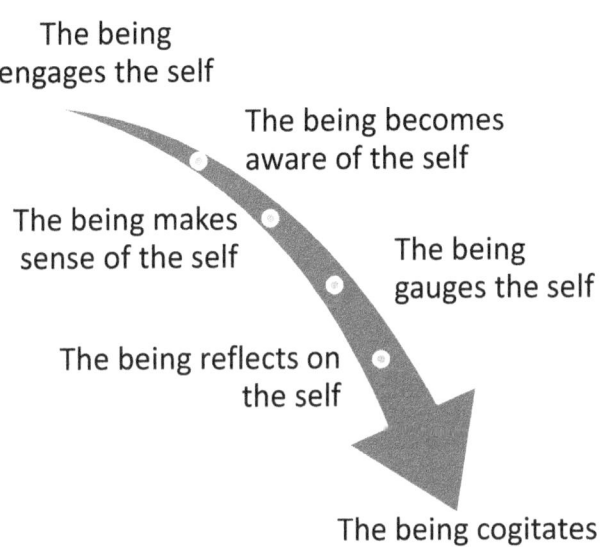

Figure 12.2: A Three-Dimensional Being and the Cogito

Controlling the Self

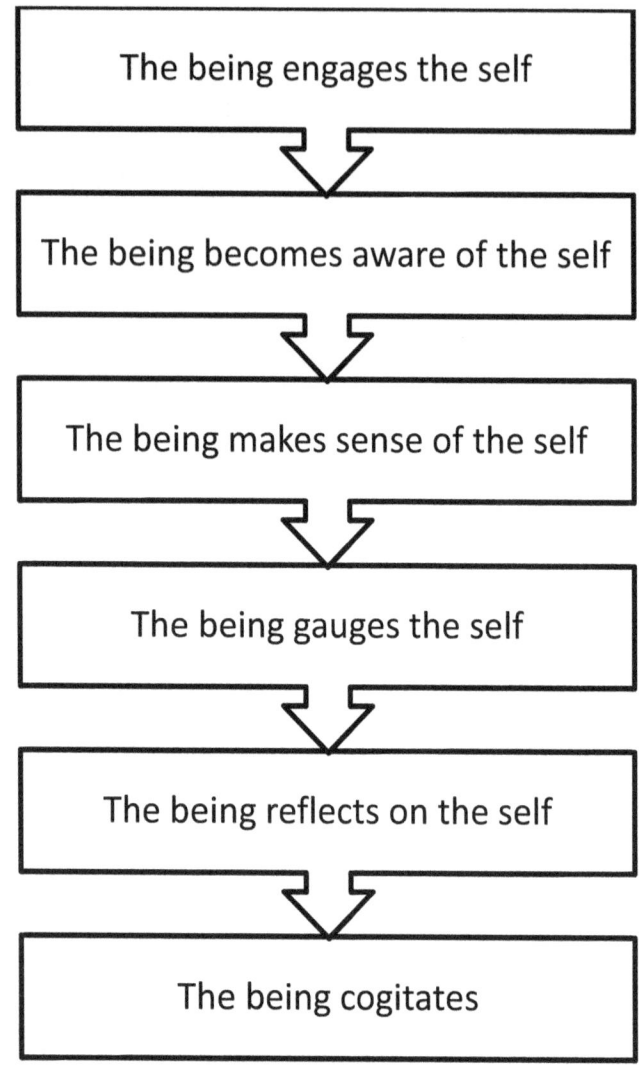

To put this idea in a more simplistic term, we could refer to this process as *Cogito Ergo Philosophus*. I should say this: I think, therefore I am. To put this view into a context, which is like René Descartes's own adumbration of this concept, we could say *Je pense, donc je philosophe*.

* * *

THINKING AND HUMAN ESSENCE

The ability to think gives essence to the being. Of course, that might not be enough to pit yourself against odds beyond luck. Despite the insights of the being about the world, the being shall strive in a similar setting. He shall do so relentlessly. He shall go all the way to guarantee himself a place to live. The being shall do so chiefly by becoming in tune with the cosmos.

Here is the problem; Human beings seldom recognize their inherent capacity to be within natural surroundings. Many people resort to various means to get to know life. Some of these methods are artificial.

To find their way, some people meditate. Others use induced hallucinations methods, techniques, or means, including, but not limited to, opiate or other

Controlling the Self

forms of drugs. Most people want to arrive at another dimension, which is seldom available by tapping on their desire to be that way. Many people gravitate towards dogma to make sense of the world or the environment in which they live.

The most obvious means that human beings have relied on as a strategy to live out without serendipity is, for lack of a better explanation, God. Of course, it is likely that God and nature are the same entity. There is no need to debate the nature of God. There is no reason to explore the roots of nature or the origins of the natural.

There is no need to point out the flaws in the notion that God—if God is or could be. God and nature are adjoining entities. God and nature live in the same plane field; they are similar.

Even if God and nature were not similar, they would be interconnected. With human survival, there could be a symbiotic link between the divine and the natural. The being shall recognize the role that both entities may play in guiding the self.

While the natural is an integral part of the being, the social environment sets up and deconstructs the being. The person—or the being—shall be aware of that reality. He shall do so at an intrinsic level.

Conclusion

Staying alive in a world designed to extirpate the man from its bowels is the bravest act a man could do both for himself and for humanity. It is an acknowledgment of one's confidence in the self. It is an act of gratitude for the self. It is a way of recognizing oneself no holds barred.

Preserving one's existence in this world is not that easy. This is hard to do. In fact, most people are likely to succumb to the blows of life. Most people are likely to falter in their search to remain a whole on planet Earth.

Faced with their calamities, some people would give up on themselves. Some of them would abandon others altogether. Some individuals, though a minority, would give up on humanity. They would become anti-humans. They would make life a

Conclusion

living hell for their fellow men. They would make life a horrible experience for other creatures.

Under the dominion of these individuals, the living experience would become a drag; it would become an incommensurable load that few people could execute their own two feet. Preserving one's existence in the world could become a task that few able-bodied men could complete on their own and for themselves.

On this rock called earth, the man is condemned to strive to remain alive. No matter what his realities are or regardless of his circumstances, the man shall preserve both his physical and mental integrity. He shall live like a man. He shall be a man. He shall exist at every turn of the treacherous road, which would drive the man to the nirvana. Of course, this is a chimerical undertaken.

The man shall never achieve his goals. He shall be nothing other than his own beingness. The man shall never know eternal peace; he shall not experience a similarity of tranquility.

The man shall be tormented forever. He shall strive, in vain, of course, to thrive. His existence shall amount to nothing but a senseless aura of vanity. The man shall struggle in futility, of course, to be anything but himself. Still, the man could only be himself. This is the essence of the misfortune of human existence. This book sought to examine this calamity from a three-dimensional lens.

The arguments that I echoed throughout this manuscript highlight the notion that a being should do everything in his power to preserve his beingness. But it might not be possible to do so all the time—and in all places. At least, this might not be conceivable beyond fortuity.

Although the act of thinking might be a trivial bodily function, every human being must do it. It is not up to the being to decide whether he should think or whether he should not do so. The being does so mechanically; he does so intrinsically. As one would expect, the being (or the man) shall do so unwittingly or unwillingly.

There is no way to separate deep thinking from simple conversations with the self. The man is constantly pondering about the self; he is constantly reflecting on his circumstances. He is relentlessly trying to figure out his place in the world where he materializes. These activities, for lack of a clear adumbration, could be understood as human reflection. The reflexive nature that is intrinsic in every living being could be described as the act of philosophizing.

I will admit that this work only scratched the surface of extremely complex ideas. The views articulated here are nowhere enough to instill a bit of clarity in the debate over the nature of humanness. It does not even provide a substantial explanation as to why men are in the world. The conversation intimated about the point of being in this world is irrefutably deficient. However, it would be erroneous to undermine the relevance of this work as the seed of other works on the same topic.

Even though this text is embryonic, its intellectual merit should not be under-appreciated. There is a need for this work. The relevance of traditional viewpoints on philosophy is fading away. It is nonsensical to continue echoing philosophical ideas that once dominated to intellectual nomenclature about human existence. By now, it should be clear to any sound-minded thinker that the world is more complex than blaming men for their own misfortunes.

The old approach to human ontology is outdated. The idea that men are free to be in a world in which they have no immediate effect is intellectually demoralizing. There is a need for a new paradigm. There is a need for a novel worldview. Here, I proposed a unique approach to the conversation. Whether I convinced you (that is, the reader) that the present scrutiny of the being is the best intellectual tool to get a serious appraisal of the reality that the being faced in his quotidian is still an open-ended question. It is certainly a question that I will you will answer for yourself.

You might agree with me that the being/the man shall preserve his beingness. Of course, he shall do so even in the face of an imminent extinction. This is the essence of human existence. The man shall persevere to be. However, to concretize this aim, the man shall be in constant communication with the natural. He shall be attuned to the world inside and outside. Hence, the man shall philosophize.

The ability of a man to think will prolong his existence in a treacherous milieu. In the same way, existence, being that of a human or any other living entity, involves the being's capacity to communicate with the natural. Philosophy is the pedestal upon which human existence rests. Therefore, for the being to be in the world, he must be aware of his beingness. That consciousness could only come from the being's concretization of where he is at a point in time and where he should be in the spectrum of his reality within the larger schema of things.

Conclusion

ABOUT THE AUTHOR

BEN WOOD JOHNSON, Ph.D.

Ben W. Johnson is an author, educator, and philosopher. He is a retired police officer. As a 27-year veteran of law enforcement, Dr. Johnson is a Fort Leonard Wood police graduate from the International Criminal Investigative Training Assistance Program (ICITAP). He is also a graduate from the Diplomatic Security Service (Mobile Division). Dr. Johnson is a retired diplomatic security officer, with expertise in close protection/presidential security, intelligence, counter ambush/terrorism, anti-riot, special weapons and tactics, and national security specialist. During his police career, Dr. Johnson held various police assignments, including patrol, anti-riot, investigation, border control, special unit response team, counter ambush, team commander, administration, scout lead driver (presidential motorcade), advanced team, counterintelligence, translator, logistics, and training.

Dr. Johnson has taught criminal justice subjects at police academies. He has taught special operations techniques to veteran police officers. Dr. Johnson is an adjunct faculty member in criminal justice at Penn State University, Harrisburg. He holds a doctorate in educational leadership and administration. His academic background includes education, law, political science, public administration, and criminal justice. His research interests include policing in America, race and crime, law, school leadership, administration, and foreign politics.

Dr. Johnson writes about legal theory, education, public policy, politics, race and crime, and ethics. He is fluent in French, Spanish, Portuguese, and Italian. He enjoys reading, poetry, painting, and music. You may contact Dr. Johnson by e-mail or via postal services. See other information below.

ALSO BY

Selected works by Dr. Ben Wood Johnson

1. Racism: What is it?
2. Sartrean Ethics: A Defense of Jean-Paul Sartre as a Moral Philosopher
3. Jean-Paul Sartre and Morality: A Legacy Under Attack
4. Sartre Lives On
5. Forced Out of Vietnam: A Policy Analysis of the Fall of Saigon
6. Natural Law: Morality and Obedience
7. Cogito Ergo Philosophus
8. Le Racisme et le Socialisme: La Discrimination Raciale dans un Milieu Capitaliste
9. International Law: The Rise of Russia as a Global Threat

Also by Ben Wood Johnson

10. Citizen Obedience: The Nature of Legal Obligation
11. Jean-Jacques Rousseau: A Collection of Short Essays
12. Être Noir : Quel Malheur !
13. L'homme et le Racisme: Être Responsable de vos Actions et Omissions
14. Pennsylvania Inspired Leadership: A Roadmap for American Educators
15. Adult Education in America: A Policy Assessment of Adult Learning
16. Striving to Survive: The Human Migration Story
17. Postcolonial Africa: Three Comparative Essays about the African State
18. Surviving the Coronavirus
19. Go Back Where You Came From
20. The Burden of Life
21. Le Fardeau de la Vie
22. How to Fix Cyberbullying: Assessing the Crisis of School Interventions
23. Why Do People Commit Crimes: Assessing Three Major Crime Theories

www.teskopublishing.com

INDEX

Ability, 24, 45, 50, 52, 57–60, 69, 74–5, 79, 141–2, 150, 156, 162
Ability to ponder, 45, 59–60
Ability to think, 24, 57–8, 79, 156
Abstract, 48, 82, 93
Abstract entity, 48
Alive, 29, 43, 52, 79, 91, 95, 98, 131, 139, 158–9
Analysis, 20, 88, 116, 136, 142
Antihumanism, 28
Anti-humans, 158
Awake, 79
Awakened, 126
Awareness, 25, 56, 92–3, 98, 100, 104, 112, 114, 125–8, 131–2, 152
Awoke, 148–9
Awoken, 58
Bear, 48, 66, 96
Bearable, 61
Bearer, 28, 43, 59, 84
Bearer of life, 59, 84
Bias, 78, 90, 108, 122
Calamity, 158, 160

Capacity, 34, 45, 50, 52, 58–60, 74, 96, 98, 104, 107, 145, 149, 156, 162
Cartesian (see: Descartes, René)
Charnel, 32, 34
Chimerical, 143, 159
Cledanor, 148–9
Coexist, 68
Cogitates, 151, 154
Cogito, 150, 152, 154, 156
Conceptualize, 58
Concretization, 162
Conversation, 50, 78–83, 88, 98, 126, 129–31, 160–1
Conversational, 81
Conversing, 79, 83, 88, 129
Creation, 44
Creatures, 41, 44–5, 53, 74, 93, 159
Danger, 56, 66, 88, 128, 131, 143
Dangerous, 30, 63, 68, 70, 128
Data, 115–7, 122, 151
Delusion, 63, 66

Index

Descartes, René, 104, 156
Dichotomous, 33
Dichotomy, 42
Dilemma, 70
Dimension, 45, 95, 102, 105, 107, 134, 157
Dimensionality, 25, 96, 132
Discovery, 122, 150
Discretion, 43
Disdain, 28
Dog-eats-dog, 69, 75
Drawbacks, 78
Drugs, 157
Opiate, 156
Earth, 29, 32, 35, 41, 46, 49, 64–5, 76–7, 158–9
Effort, 29, 71, 90, 143, 149
Endure, 30, 57, 142
Engage, 58, 81–2, 94, 121, 151–2, 154
Engages in the cogito, 152
Engages in thinking, 151
Epistemology, 30, 78
Ergo (see: Cogito)
Escape, 141
Esteem, 64
Excogitate, 45
Existentialism, 20, 25, 121
Existentialist, 121
Existing, 77
Exogenous, 63, 137
Factuality, 34
Fallibility, 68
Fluidity, 34
Foolishness, 75
Forego, 70
Fortuity, 71, 160
Fortunes, 60

Foundation, 33, 40, 45, 49, 53, 59–60, 66, 140
Fragility, 98
Free, 121, 161
Freedom, 25, 65, 89, 121
Freewill, 43
Full-body, 35
Gauge, 45, 108, 118, 131, 140, 152, 154
Gaze, 109, 114, 116–8
Gazing, 106, 114–6, 118–9, 124
Genuine, 32, 51, 142
Geography, 143
Glass, 109
Global, 97
Glorification, 68
God, 64, 68, 78, 157
Dogma, 157
Gratitude, 158
Habitat, 75
Hair, 96
Hairbrush, 95–6
Hairstyle, 117
Half, 126
Half-abstract, 148
Half-physical, 148
Hallucinations, 156
Happiness, 69
Harmony, 63
Haughtiness, 77
Hubris, 75, 77
Humanism, 20
Humanistic, 45
Humanity, 35, 42, 57, 63, 75, 158
Humankind, 44, 64, 75

Humanness, 25, 28, 30, 42–3, 49–51, 62, 66, 79, 161
Humanoid, 62, 78
Hurdles, 30, 49
Illogical, 68, 75
Illusion, 92, 118
Illusory, 70, 92, 121
Imaginable, 69, 129
Impulse, 142–3
Individual, 33, 40, 50, 66, 68, 71–2, 89, 92, 107, 142, 158–9
Instinct, 141–2
Instinctively, 106, 144
Interpretation, 109
Intimate, 92
Introspection, 25, 112
Introspective, 45, 52, 62, 94, 108, 121, 138, 150
Intrusive, 131
Intuition, 141
Irrationality, 89
Jargons, 30
Jealous, 30
Journey, 64, 75
Jungle, 143
Kernel, 52
Kind, 28, 34, 53, 59, 64–5, 75, 136
Kindly, 64
Knowledge, 74, 94, 108, 117, 119, 131, 149–50
Leopard, 143
Lethal, 24, 56, 63, 68, 70, 143
Lethargic, 33
Liberty, 65, 69
Livingness, 131
Locus, 36
Lost, 67, 81, 91, 93, 100, 122
Luck, 58, 156
Machine, 43
Mammals, 76
Maniacal, 91
Manifest, 32
Manipulate, 121, 124
Mars, 35, 75, 77
Material, 20, 45, 136, 138
Materializes, 160
Mechanical, 20
Mechanism, 122, 148, 150
Mental, 82, 159
Metaphysical, 45, 51
Milieu, 28–9, 32–3, 35–6, 45, 56, 60, 63, 71, 78, 83, 139, 144, 149–50, 162
Mirror, 25–6, 101–4, 106, 108–10, 119, 124–5, 137–8, 140
Misconceptions, 64
Misery, 66
Misfortune, 107, 159, 161
Misgivings, 91
Moribund, 43
Motion, 116, 119
Multidimensional, 82
Multitasking, 81
Multi-thinking, 81
Mundane, 49
Mystery, 41, 58, 77
Naturally, 89
Naturalness, 34
Nirvana, 159
Nonliving, 44–5
Non-physical, 48
Nonsensical, 66, 161
Norms, 88

Index

Obedience, 68
Object, 41, 43–4, 88, 95–6
Objective, 116
Ontology, 20, 42, 161
  Ontological, 42, 51
Ordinary, 24, 74, 76
Organism, 44
Origins, 68, 157
Overpower, 89–90
Overwhelmed, 129
Paradigm, 41, 161
Pathogens, 143
Patrick, 22, 116–9
Pervasive, 28
Perversions, 65
Phenomenology, 20
Philosophe, 156
Philosophical, 29–30, 161
Philosophize, 45, 150, 152, 162
Philosophizing, 51, 150–2, 160
Philosophus, 156
Philosophy, 20, 141, 150, 161–2
Physical, 34–5, 42, 48, 82, 91, 93–5, 97, 108–10, 125, 135–6, 148–9, 159
Physiological, 53
Ponder, 24, 45, 59–60, 62, 98, 129, 150
  Pondering, 151, 160
Precocity, 28, 143
Preconceived, 33, 103, 106, 117–9
Precondition, 70, 149
Prejudice, 50
Premature, 122, 129
Prematurely, 29

Preserving, 71, 98, 129, 141–2, 158–9
Pro-choice, 79
Pro-life, 79
Psyche, 67
Psychologically, 108
Pursuit, 65, 105
Quash, 89
Quintessence, 45, 61, 150
Quintessential, 144
Quotidian, 53, 57, 60, 161
Ramifications, 58, 72
Random, 67
Rational, 64–6
Readjustment, 126
Reason, 53, 58–9, 91, 105, 121–2, 134, 143, 157
Reclusion, 66
Recourse, 71
Robot, 44
Robotized, 24, 44
Romantic, 64
Rousseau, Jean-Jacques, 64
Savages, 64
Self-awareness, 24–5, 54, 58, 98, 128
  Self-discovery, 58, 104, 108
  Self-preservation, 31
Self-within-the-self, 18, 26, 48, 88, 122, 134, 136, 138–42, 145, 148–9
Serendipitous, 57
Serendipity, 31, 57, 157
Stimuli, 129
Stimulus, 121
Subconscious, 92, 126
Subconsciously, 80, 106, 110
Subconsciousness, 141

Subject, 44
Subjective, 50–1, 109, 116
Subjectivity, 118
Subliminally, 129
Sublingual, 79
Sublunary, 149
Subsist, 28, 68
Subsistence, 50
Subsisting, 28
Superfluous, 78
Superhumans, 46
Supermen, 74
Survival, 29–30, 46, 49, 52–3, 56–7, 68–71, 74–5, 105, 130, 141, 144, 157
Survivalist, 57
Survive, 29–30, 69, 71–2, 143–4, 151
Surviving, 52, 144
Survivor, 52
Symbiosis, 83
Symbiotic, 137, 157
Synthesis, 122
Synthesize, 117, 119
Theoretical, 51
Theorists, 64, 121
Theorize, 45
Theorizing, 51
Thinker, 50, 64–5, 76, 161
Thinking, 26, 45, 50, 52–3, 58–62, 67, 75, 81, 94, 151–2, 156, 160
Thought, 31, 45, 50, 52–3, 62, 64, 76, 79
Thoughtful, 62
Thought producing, 53
Three-dimensional, 24–5, 42, 45, 48–9, 82–4, 96–8, 104–5, 114, 119, 122, 134–5, 154, 160
Three-dimensionality, 25, 48–9, 81, 84, 97
Thyself, 104, 152
Tranquility, 65, 121, 159
Transcend, 33–4, 50
Treacherous, 56, 65, 159, 162
True, 33, 35, 40, 44, 49, 58, 94, 107, 109, 120
Truth, 40
Trust, 64
Two-dimensional, 24, 40–4, 48, 96, 102, 106, 124
Two-dimensionality, 31, 43, 96
Unabridged-body, 35
Unaware, 148
Un-barbarized, 45
Unidirectional, 49
Uniqueness, 76
Un-robotized, 45
Un-streamlined, 45
Unthinking, 44
Untrue, 43
Valuable, 50, 93
Value, 93
Vanity, 159
Verbiage, 50
Vessel, 108, 136
Vice, 83, 96
Vicissitudes, 30
Victim, 65
Victimized, 143
Vulnerabilities, 143
Wake, 148
Watching, 25, 102–3, 109, 125
Whole-body, 35
Wilderness, 56, 75

Index

Young, 117–9, 148–9
You-within-you, 82
You-yourself, 138

www.ingramcontent.com/pod-product-compliance
Lightning Source LLC
Chambersburg PA
CBHW022106040426
42451CB00007B/139